Two Minute Warning

TWO MINUTE WARNING

Why It's TIME TO HONOR Jewish People...
Before The Clock Runs Out

*On the Possibilities of End-Time
Authentic Christianity*

Coach Bill McCartney
and
Aaron Fruh

VMI Publishers
Sisters, Oregon

Published by
VMI Publishers
Sisters, Oregon
www.vmipublishers.com

ISBN: 1935265008
ISBN 13: 9781935265009
Library of Congress Control Number: 2009926354

Printed in the USA.

Cover design by Kirk DouPonce, DogEared Design

TABLE OF CONTENTS

DEDICATIONS

I dedicate this book to the love of my life – Lyndi.
She is the most unselfish, giving person I have ever met.
Within the depths of her heart is a pure love for Jewish people.
Lyndi, thank you for pursuing this vision with me.

I also dedicate this book to four Jewish believers who have
impacted my life with wisdom and grace:

My pastor, Rabbi Gene Binder, who continues to
nourish my soul with wise counsel.
Rabbi Michael Walker, who combines humility
and grace – He is a genuine shepherd.
Rabbi Jonathan Bernis lavishes scholarship
and prudence upon me.
Rabbi Aaron Fruh, my co-author, is whole-hearted
and truly genuine. He put me on his shoulders
and carried this book to the finish.

— *Coach Mac*
Bill McCartney

I dedicate this book to my wife, Sharon, with whom
I look forward to growing old, while remaining young.
Atem maor einye – You are the light of my eyes.

And to my children, Rachel, Elizabeth, Hannah, and Nathan,
for your warm searching hearts. *Ahuvaie, ani ohav otchem* –
My dears, I love you.

—*Aaron Fruh*

PREFACE

This book can only be read effectively in the power of the Holy Spirit. It will startle, awaken, and educate the believer. The time has come in God's providence for a true reckoning with our history. The body of Christ has been divided for 1,900 years. Only a Holy Spirit driven account of the past can build a bridge to the present.

May I suggest that the reader stop and be searched. Do you have any sin that has not been confessed? Ask the Holy Spirit to wash you whiter than snow. Read this book in a state of repentance. This will prepare your heart for the difficult days ahead. Essentially, the person God calls "loyal" is the one who hears and obeys the Word of God in the power of the Holy Spirit. This book rallies around the very things God's Word instructs us to do in this hour.

The proof of this assertion and those who read and respond in the power of the Holy Spirit will unite and ignite the church in these last days. Read and respond! Be propelled forward with vigor and resolve.

Bill McCartney

Acknowledgments

We want to express our deep appreciation
to the following people:

Dr. Raleigh Washington for his steadfast loyalty to
Coach McCartney. Sincere thanks are also in order for
Rabbi Steven Barack, Don Finto, Dan Juster, Evan Levine,
Dr. Grant Osborne, Rabbi Russ Resnik and Dr. Paul Tinlin for
their very helpful critiques of the manuscript.

We also want to thank Bill Carmichael and his team at VMI
Publishers for their willingness to take on this project and for
their professionalism. Special thanks is expressed to Lacey Hanes
Ogle, Associate Publisher/Senior Editor of VMI, for her dedicated
work and expression of grace as we pressed the envelope
on our deadlines. Much appreciation also goes to Lynn Lindquist
for her commitment to read through the manuscript three times –
offering constructive ideas and critiques.

Lastly, we want to give huge applause to Lyndi McCartney
(Bill's wife) for managing all of the many e-mails that flooded
her computer – often on a daily basis. Lyndi, we would
not have made it without you!

Two Minute Warning

*No man can struggle with advantage against the spirit
of his age and country, and however powerful a man may be,
it is hard for him to make his contemporaries share feelings
and ideas which run counter to the general run
of their hopes and desires.*
Alexis De Tocqueville

You are a part of a generation of intimacy seekers. Our culture desperately longs for a depth in relationships that goes beyond the mundane and the superficial. At the root of this quest for reality and transparency is a longing in our souls to know the living God and to be known by Him. Because of this need to find the reality of who God is and what He requires of us, many in our generation are pursuing intimacy with God with reckless abandon. A new purity of heart is being expressed through our worship. Think of the new movements that have as their main purpose the desire to find the heart of the Lord of heaven: The Call, Passion Conferences, International House of Prayer—and the list goes on. No doubt something is happening. Things are changing.

1

This is not a book about football. Because you may remember me as the head football coach at the University of Colorado, it would be natural for you to think that it would be. As well, this is not a book *about* men. Again, it would be natural for you to think that because of my long association with the Promise Keepers Movement as its founder.

Yes, by nature I am a person that has carried in his heart a passion to see stadiums filled with men worshiping Jesus. Also, by nature and calling, I've coached football teams and enjoyed a degree of success. I love the game, and coaching at the collegiate level was a passion of mine. Because I left coaching at a fairly young age, a lot of people ask me if I intend to coach again. This book is, in part, the answer to that question. The concepts found on the pages before you are so vital that I have dedicated the rest of my life to pursue them as one would a buried treasure. It is my hope that the discovery of this treasure will be a pursuit worthy of your life's attention as well.

By trade I was a football coach. When you are in the game as long as I have been, you can never shake the title *Coach*. I think my strongest spiritual gifting is encouragement. I am not a preacher. I am a "reacher." A "reacher" encourages and exhorts. He challenges, rallies, and compels. He asks people to reach deeper and give more even when they think they have already given their all. As the founder of Promise Keepers, I am leading a national men's movement rather than directing plays on the gridiron, yet people still address me as *Coach*. I think they are simply calling out my gift of encouragement.

Because I am a football coach by trade and an encourager by heart, you will have to excuse the fact that when I think about life, it's generally through the metaphor of football. As a Christian, I believe in the soon appearance of Jesus Christ. Bible prophecy experts tell us that on the prophetic time clock we are just two minutes from the midnight hour—the time of Christ's appearance. In the National Football League, when the two minute warning alarm sounds off, it stops the game clock. The warning serves as a checkpoint to let both teams know that mere moments remain. When a game is close in score, the two minute warning sends a clear message: "This is it! Play with desperation! Fight for every inch. Only seconds remain!"

Many football games are decided in the declining seconds. Routinely, coaches practice these decisive situations over and over. Strategy is thoroughly implemented depicting real game situations. Does he need one or two touchdowns or just a field goal to win the game? Furthermore, he drills his team on how to protect a lead when they possess the ball. It takes careful execution to bleed the clock. In the final two minutes a coach tends to play only those players who demonstrate great poise and maturity so that unnecessary mistakes or penalties won't influence the outcome. Can his team march down the field with no timeouts available? When should they get out of bounds to stop the clock? Coaches remind their squads that only the best conditioned teams can rise up to secure victory as the clock ticks to zero. The best prepared teams relish those opportunities when the game is on the line!

My Single Greatest Victory

At Colorado, the single greatest victory I enjoyed took place in my thirteenth and final year as head coach. We were playing the University of Michigan in Ann Arbor. Previously, I had been an assistant coach at Michigan for eight and a half years. Michigan had won more games than any other team in college football history. It was early in the season. Both teams were undefeated and ranked in the top ten nationally. Michigan led twenty-six to twenty-one with two minutes remaining in the game. They had the ball on offense and we used our remaining timeouts to stop the clock in hopes of one more offensive possession. Finally, they punted the ball to us, where we fair caught it, inside our own twenty yard line. With just fifteen seconds left on the clock, how could we negotiate the ball more than eighty yards up the field?

On the sidelines, our offensive coaches instructed our offensive unit that we had enough time for only two plays. The first play would need to move us up field far enough so that the final play could be a pass that could be thrown all the way into the end zone. We had to score a touchdown to win. Sure enough, we completed a pass for a first down that stopped the clock on our own thirty-three yard line. Our quarterback was told to heave the ball as far as he could with as much trajectory as possible. This would permit our receivers to sprint sixty-seven yards to the goal line. In addition, the receivers were told to deflect the ball in the air if they couldn't catch it themselves.

This was a play we practiced every Thursday before the game the following Saturday. Everyone knew what to do. They realized that this was a very difficult play to pull off. Rarely had it worked on Thursdays! Yet, as 107,000 fans in the stadium and millions more on television watched, we scored on that play and won the game twenty-seven to twenty-six. The date was September 24, 1994. Yes, we were extremely fortunate. But, we were also fully prepared.

Responding to the Pressures of the Times

How do you respond when the pressure is on? Surely, we define ourselves by our ability to meet life's challenges. There is a graphic parallel here. Don't miss it! As a believer, recognize that the days are darkening and that crunch time is surfacing. These are warnings!

I am not a theologian. As I've said, I'm a football coach. But from everything happening in our world today, I'm convinced that mere moments remain before God the Father brings closure to time as we know it. Radical Islam accounts for twenty percent of the world's 1.2 billion Muslims. By my calculations that's 240 million committed Muslims who are willing to die for their beliefs—nearly the size of the population of the United States. On top of that, radical rogue nations are going nuclear. At the time of writing this book in the spring of 2009, our nation is facing a serious financial crisis. The world markets are collapsing and governments are taking control of the banking system. What lies ahead for us? Have we entered into the birth pangs that the Scriptures promise the last days will produce? If so, what preparations are we making for crunch time? Are we ready for earth's coming night? Have we come prepared to win? Is our head in the game? Are we focused on Christ and His Kingdom? Are we pursuing God's purpose like desperate men and women in the final two minutes of a championship game?

When I was preparing the Colorado Buffalos to face Notre Dame for the national championship, I never told the players in the preceding week, "Listen guys, don't be concerned about this game. I can tell you factually that Notre Dame is only good for three quarters. Right before the game gets intense at the beginning of the fourth quarter, their coach will call the entire team off of the field, and they will head to the safety of the locker room. We will win by default, so there's no need to push hard in practice this week. In fact, I'm giving you the day off today!"

What coach would be so presumptuous to say such things? Even if he had inside information that the other team would forfeit, a good coach would never tell that to his team—especially before a national championship! A true coach would push his team to the limit in pre-game preparation and strategy. An experienced coach knows that his inside information about the other team's strategy, weak spots, or degree of injuries could be wrong. A good coach would make sure his team was one hundred percent prepared to face the opposition, even if the press voted his team the favorite. As a coach I learned that in football, there is no substitute for vigilant, disciplined preparation.

In the last several years, many Bible prophecy teachers have concluded that we need not prepare for the coming desperate days. No intense planning and preparedness will be necessary, they tell us. They say with assured confidence that right before the game gets really intense, the Lord is going to blow the whistle and pull us off the field to the safety of the locker room. Again, please remember that I am not a theologian. I am a football coach asking a simple question: wouldn't it be wiser to prepare for the entire endgame in case our inside information is incorrect?

My personal belief is that God the Father has kept the time of the Lord's appearance a mystery, and He wants to keep it that way. He is a wonderful battle strategist and does not want to let the enemy in on His plans, so He has purposefully cloaked the timing of His coming. I believe that the Father is not concerned about us knowing exactly *when* His Son is appearing—but that His Son *is* appearing. In turn, He has given us an awesome pre-game strategy to help prepare us for anything. The Scriptures teach us to prepare vigilantly and soberly for the days of perplexity that lie ahead. This book is a playbook manual that will prepare you for the final two minutes—come what may.

In this book, I want to be a coach of encouragement to you. I want to prepare you for the championship game—all four quarters. I want to rally and compel you to reach deeper, even if you think you are already giving your all. Your family needs you to be ready, vigilant, watchful, and prepared—come what may, rather than trusting wholeheartedly in theories that promise a way out of the intensity of earth's final moments. Coaches, as I said, always play the most mature, seasoned players in the final seconds of the game. Don't think it is any coincidence that the Lord has placed you on earth at this time. He chose you because He knew you would be prepared when the heat is on!

Called to Finish Strong

It should not come as a surprise that a football coach would concern himself with end-time events. Coaches invest their careers in finishing strong. Early in the season, the best coaches know intuitively what the end looks like. Routinely, they envision the changes and progress needed to contend for the title. Proverbs 29:18 says: "Where there is no revelation, the people cast off restraint." This Scripture can easily be understood to mean: "When a person can't see the prize, they won't pay the price." Christ Himself speaks of this prize in Revelation 21:7: "He who overcomes shall inherit all things, and I will be his God and he shall be My son."

You and I are called to finish strong! This is our greatest challenge, and it is something we should see clearly, show creatively, and say constantly! We are called to overcome no matter how intense the pressures of life are. Paul the apostle made this very clear: "For this reason I also suffer these things; nevertheless I am not ashamed, for I know whom I have believed and am persuaded that He is able to keep what I have committed to Him until that Day" (2 Tim. 1:12). I think about that "Day" everyday. Of course, I'm referencing the "Day" when I will stand before the Lord to give an account of what I did with what He gave me. No doubt, my record as a coach will have no value on "that Day." Rather, did I intimately know Him, and did I make Him known? Did I pursue His will with utmost loyalty? These are issues of primary importance to the King of creation.

Seventy-three Words That Will Change the World

One way to discover the heart of God is to listen to the prayers of His Son. One of the most important prayers of Jesus is the central focus of this book. It's the prayer that He prayed in John chapter 17 at the conclusion of the Last Supper. At the end of the meal, Jesus lifted up His eyes to heaven and audibly prayed. This significant prayer is known as the high priestly prayer of our Lord. Jesus prayed this prayer in pure Hebraic style—passionately and audibly, because He wanted it to be heard and recorded. It was a very important prayer.

Could there be something of eternal value we have missed in Jesus' high priestly prayer? Could there be a mandate He proclaimed within His concluding prayer that is a key element in His eternal plan to reconcile all things to Himself? I believe there is. In fact, there are three verses within this prayer that include seventy-three words so crucial that if they are not answered, the future outpouring of the glory of God we long for will never be fully manifested. In these seventy-three words Jesus unveils His eternal purpose. Here are the seventy-three words from John 17:

V. 20: I do not pray for these alone, but also for those who will believe in Me through their word;

V. 21: that they all may be one, as You, Father, are in Me, and I in You; that they also may be one in Us, that the world may believe that You sent Me.

V. 22: And the glory which You gave Me I have given them, that they may be one just as We are one.

Please read v. 20 once again. Let me ask a question: who are "these," and who are "those"? "These" would be the twelve Jewish disciples, the seventy Jewish leaders that Jesus sent out two by two, and the gathering of His Jewish followers that had come to faith in Him. Who then are "those"? "Those" would be the people from the world who would believe in Him. From a biblical perspective there are two kinds of people in the world: Jews and people outside of the Jewish community—Gentiles. "These" then are Jewish believers and "Those" are gentile believers.

The deep significance of what Jesus is praying comes in the first six words of verse 21: "That they all may be one." Jews and Gentiles worshiping Jesus as one? Yes, and even more significantly, Jesus prays that this restored relationship through Messiah would be the key that would bring the world to Him: "That the world may believe that

You sent Me" (v. 21). In effect, Jesus is saying that when these two people who have had an historic enmity heal the divide and become one, the world will then experience its final harvest of souls. An amazing promise is found in verse 22: "And the glory which You gave Me I have given them." God's glory is only poured out in full measure on "them"—Jews and Gentiles together as one—not as two separate people. The world has never experienced the full outpouring of this glory because this prayer of Jesus has yet to be fully answered. As well, it is only through this outpouring of God's glory upon both Jew and Gentile that provides the possibility of oneness and unity: "And the glory which You gave Me I have given them, that they may be one just as We are one" (v. 22).

A Promise of Incredible Glory

The Hebrew word for glory is *kavod*, and it means "weightiness" or "heaviness." It describes the splendor and power of the tangible presence of God. The glory that the living God poured out upon His Son was so powerful and "weighty" that demons trembled in His presence. This same kavod left the disciples speechless on the Mount of Transfiguration. It was this glory that caused Lazarus to walk out of a dead man's tomb after four days. It was kavod that caused a platoon of soldiers to fall backwards when they approached Jesus in the Garden of Gethsemane and a large number of hardened Roman guards to fall like dead men at His resurrection. It was kavod that caused astonishment in twelve fishermen when Jesus rose up in a storm tossed boat to rebuke the sea of Galilee. This same glory opened blind eyes and deaf ears and caused those possessed of the devil to be clothed and put into their right minds. And, it was this glory that gave Jesus authority when He spoke of the things of God.

This glory has never fully been expressed in the earth because Jew and Gentile have never fully become one in Messiah. The world is waiting for this divide to be healed. Like you, I pray for the day when every knee bows before the Lord of glory. But only kavod—

9

the "weighty" glory of God, will cause the full scale bowing that we Christians long to see in an unbelieving world. As Jew and Gentile become one, the same manifest kavod of the living God which He poured upon His Son will be poured upon us! When this divide is healed, the powerful manifestation of God's glory will descend upon the earth in such tangible "weighty" proportions that unbelievers will bow, the sick will be healed, and the dead will rise. If you long for this day, you are reading the right book.

A Great Divide That Must Be Healed

We will see in this book that for the past 1,900 years, Satan has caused a great divide between Jews and Gentiles. He knows when these seventy-three words of intercession are fulfilled his kingdom will crumble. When the kavod of God descends upon Jewish and Gentiles together as one in Messiah, cities and nations will bow under the weight of its splendor. Our adversary the devil has mustered his armies to keep Jews and Gentiles separate in order to keep the glory from being fully manifested in the earth. That's why you can look back over the last 1,900 years of the history of the church and see the murderous violence it employed against the Jews. Satan himself has been the architect of this wide gulf between Jew and Gentile. But things are changing! There are numerous supernatural signs that the gorge is narrowing. This book tells the story of the divide and proclaims the hope of its destined restoration and the glory that will follow. Your future destiny is directly connected to the healing of this age long broken relationship between Jew and Gentile. The impartation of the same glory the Father gave His Son awaits this reconciliation. This is the final hour. It is a moment that requires true loyalty to the Word of God. Because Jesus declared in His high priestly prayer that the key to the end-time outpouring of His manifest glory was the joining of Jews and Gentiles as one in God, we should follow

His lead and join with Him on earth as He prays in heaven: "May they be one!" True loyalty to the Lord is simply this: To hear and obey His Word in the power of the Holy Spirit. Jesus said in Matthew 7:24: "Therefore whoever hears these sayings of Mine, and does them, I will liken him to a wise man who built his house on the rock." To have a rock-like faith that stands the tempest and storm of this final hour will require not only hearing God's Word but obeying it.

I believe that if you could visit heaven today you would hear these seventy-three words from the high priestly prayer of Jesus still emanating from the throne room with loud cries in a spirit of travail. I believe Jesus consistently lifts His voice and prays to the Father, "May they be one"! He continually offers this prayer of intercession because Jews and Gentiles have yet to become one. In His eternal priesthood, He continues to stand in the gap in order to heal this age long divide. He knows that the world hangs in the balance so He continually prays these seventy-three world changing words. The Lord of Glory is presently shaking things up in order to bring about their fulfillment.

Earth's Coming Three Revolutions

In football, the defensive team's main role is to defend their field position and cause a turnover, which would give the offense the ball back in scoring position. The word *turnover* can be defined as change, shakeup, transfer, or revolution. In this book, I want to unveil to you three approaching revolutions—turnovers or changes—that Jesus is sending to His church: the revolution of separation, the revolution of restoration, and the revolution of preparation.

The one constant the future holds is change. Jesus is preparing to restructure and refit His church so that His end-time purposes can be accomplished. Three earthquake-like revolutions of significant magnitude are coming to the body of Christ. Their residual tremors will be felt the world over. Shakeup is imminent. Things are changing.

The Lord is calling out the overcomers. These are fully prepared believing saints who, like Esther of old, understand they "have come to the kingdom for such a time as this" (Esther 4:14).

Father God has matured this God-fearing righteous remnant for this final hour. They have quietly served the Lord and His people. They are intercessors. They have understanding of the times. They are kingdom people who are longing for the appearance of the Lord. Like the miracle of the water being turned to wine in Cana of Galilee, the Lord has saved the best until last. Now, when the two minute warning alarm has sounded, the King of creation is rallying His seasoned end-time remnant to fulfill His eternal plan. Only those who see the prize and are willing to pay the price will be able to stand in this dark hour.

This is why it is important that we prepare now for what may very possibly lie ahead. These three revolutions are coming. You can be sure of it. They are life changing. The prophet Daniel speaks of a last day's remnant of bold saints that have a clear understanding of God's end-time purposes: "...But the people who know their God shall be strong, and carry out great exploits. And those of the people who understand shall instruct many" (Dan. 11:32–33).

What exactly are these three revolutions about? How do I embrace them? Just how did a football coach come to discover these three world changing revolutions? God cheers when His wonders are worked through simple people.

My Story

What if God revealed something to you that you had never seen before? Would you pursue it? Would you immerse yourself in it until it became a part of your daily walk with Jesus? What if the thing God showed you He wanted you to embrace was foolish—even despised? Would you receive it or discard it with embarrassment? Would you be loyal to the Father? Such were the questions I faced when the Lord first revealed the three coming revolutions to me from the Scriptures. However, it became very clear to me that these three coming revolutions would become the centerpiece of God's end-time purpose. Up front I will tell you this: earth's final harvest depends on whether or not we embrace them. For the last five years I have been on a sojourn of discovery—a journey into the very heart of God the Father.

Initially, when Promise Keepers started gathering men, it was clear to me that the Lord instructed us to rally those who had been "born-again" of the Holy Spirit. It was imperative to emphasize that God was calling men together across all boundaries. This included the most conservative to the most prophetic. Black, brown, red, yellow, and white men were to be invited. The young and elderly should feel welcome as well. We were to show no preferences to the wealthy and the economically privileged. Truly, it was intended to be a massive bonding over the broad cross section of the brotherhood of believers.

Early on, Isaiah 40:5 jumped out at me: "The glory of the Lord shall be revealed, and all flesh shall see it together." I've learned that when the Word of God is spoken, read or heard, and the Spirit of God takes the Word of God and strikes fire, there will be change. Truthfully, this describes the impact I experience to this day when this verse is proclaimed. Certainly, I have the strongest sense that we are fast approaching the depth of Isaiah 40:5 becoming a reality soon and very soon.

The moment that God first revealed His heart to me and showed me these coming three revolutions was in Phoenix, Arizona in February of 2003. Promise Keepers hosted about ten thousand clergy. The theme "Come Near To Me," taken from Genesis 45:4, reminded the leaders of Joseph humbly embracing his brothers who years earlier betrayed him by selling him into slavery.

The first evening was set aside for a presentation by the Messianic Jewish community (these are Jewish leaders who acknowledge Jesus as Lord and Savior). They humbly encouraged gentile believers to recognize and appreciate them as they maintained their Jewish distinctive. Collectively, they enlisted us to "come near." Together, we fulfilled the "one new man" (Jew and Gentile as one in Jesus) Ephesians chapters 2 and 3 introduce.

The next day was devoted to Jewish and gentile believers coming together as one. Personally, I was enriched and found the overall scope riveting. Upon returning to Denver from the conference, I began receiving letters from Christian leaders who had attended the Phoenix event. Their comments concerned me. They did not feel that the call to reconciliation at the conference was appropriate. I soon discovered that some of the authors of these letters held a view concerning Jewish people known as: "Replacement Theology," "Supercessionism," or "Triumphalism." This is the belief that God has cancelled His eternal covenants with the Jewish people, and now the gentile church is the "new Israel" of God. According to Triumphalism, the Jews are no longer on God's radar. Gentile Christians are now the "chosen" and Jews have been forever rejected by God.

Remember, I'm a football coach not a theologian. I knew that what we had done in Phoenix had honored God. I was unaware that a deep divide existed between Christians and Jews. Consequently, I felt the Lord prompting me to go into the waiting room (a prolonged season of prayer) to gain understanding concerning these things. Isaiah 40:31 says: "Those who wait on the Lord shall renew their strength; they shall mount up with wings like eagles, they shall run and not be weary, they shall walk and not faint."

Waiting is Unhurried Pursuit

In this context "wait" is unhurried pursuit. Be ready to move at any moment, but maintain that posture should God tarry. An eagle can soar to ten thousand feet. In a dive he can fly at speeds reaching two hundred miles an hour. He has a panoramic view. He is above his enemies. He can see a rabbit from high altitude with razor vision—that's dinner. He can spot a fox—that's the enemy. When a storm comes, the eagle embraces the thermal currents of the wind by "mounting" up with his huge wingspan. He flies directly into the storm as it propels him higher. When we "wait" upon the Lord He equips us for our next assignment.

I spent precisely nine months in the "waiting room." On December 13, 2003, friends from San Diego mailed a plane ticket inviting me to California to share what God had been saying to me as I waited on Him. This was the profound timing of God. Everyone knows nine months is the length of time we wait for new birth. When I arrived in San Diego and sat down with these godly friends, I shared what the Lord had birthed in my heart during my time alone with Him.

Proverbs 4:18 says: "But the path of the just is like the shining sun, that shines ever brighter unto the perfect day." This is a picture of the sun released in full power. It teaches that a believer's life unfolds sequentially. All that has happened is in preparation for what is next—and what is next is truly powerful. I shared with these friends that in my time alone with God I was captured by the prayer of Jesus in John 17:20–22 (the seventy-three words in Jesus' high priestly prayer I shared early on in this chapter). I shared with them that I believed Jesus was telling His disciples the key to world harvest is when Jewish and gentile people, who share their common faith in Jesus, get together! As we have seen, one of Satan's chief objectives is to make sure this relationship is never birthed. The world has not witnessed the powerful supernatural expression of this relationship for nearly 1,900 years. Satan has cunningly separated us by jealousy, hatred, and fear. Yet, in the infinite wisdom of God, He has chosen the wild olive shoots (gentile believers) to be grafted into the same olive tree as the natural branches (Israel) and receive the nourishing sap of the spiritual commonwealth of Israel. In this book we will see that through this fully restored relationship, the glory of God will be manifested upon the earth with such magnitude that signs, wonders, and miracles will be commonplace. Multitudes of souls will also be swept into the Kingdom of God in a final harvest of souls.

God's Game Plan for the End of the Age

This is God's plan. This is what Jesus prayed in John 17. And He has never prayed a prayer that has not been answered. This is God's prescription for worldwide revival. Zechariah 8:23 says: "In those days ten men from every language of the nations shall grasp the sleeve of a Jewish man saying, 'Let us go with you for we have heard that God is with you.'"

This day is being ushered in. We need our Jewish brothers and sisters to model what earlier generations were taught. The church of the first century was built on the foundation of Hebrew apostles and prophets. The teaching of the church was centered on Hebraic ideals of family life, prayer, holiness, community, and ministering to the needs of the poor.

In this book we are going to discuss God's final game plan for the end of the age. The book serves as a warning of what is to come. These three revolutions that are coming to the earth all have to do with the age long relationship between Christians and Jews. That God would choose this restored relationship as the key to end-time blessing and harvest may seem foolish. Yet, the foolishness of God is wiser than man's strength (1 Cor. 1:26–29).

I am co-authoring this book with Aaron David Fruh. Aaron is a pastor, author, and also a Jewish believer. I must be frank with you: The things we are saying in this book will be quite shocking and disturbing to you. In the first half of the book we examine the long history of Christian violence toward Jewish people. Before we can move on to restoration and reconciliation, we must come to terms with our collective past. Be assured, it's not pretty. The second half of the book is restorative and redemptive and unveils the wonderful blessing you will receive when the relationship with Jewish people is restored. Dear reader, we make this bold promise to you up front: If you are willing to embrace the coming three revolutions found in this book, the glory (kavod) of the Father in heaven will descend

16

upon your life and family in a way you have never experienced before. We have experienced this as the truths in this book have been unfolded.

For me, this has been a five year journey into the heart of the Father. You are about to embark on this life changing journey with me. We begin in a part of history that many in the church would like to avoid—The Holocaust. Our first stop will be to a concentration camp covered in white ash—Auschwitz. Prepare yourself because this is not going to be easy.

PART I:

The Revolution of Separation

Endless Night

Hence today I believe that I am acting in accordance with the will of the Almighty Creator: by defending myself against the Jew, I am fighting for the work of the Lord.

Adolph Hitler
Mein Kampf

Whoever kills you will think he is offering a service to God.

Jesus
John 16:2

It was a pleasure burning the chosen. The ashes of fiddlers, rabbis, doctors, scientists, artists, and philosophers—the greatest minds of Europe—danced heavenward along mortar lines of the brick chimneys in Auschwitz. Generations present and future vanquished by fire. Little white shards of smoldering Jewish flesh and bone rose past church steeple, bell tower, and cross—forming forever a cloud of witnesses. The crematoriums at the death camps blanketed surrounding hamlets with human ash fine as freshly fallen snow—endless winter. In Auschwitz alone, two million people were gassed and burned between May 1941 and the end of 1943. For those who survived the Holocaust—the mass murder of over six million Jewish innocents—

life for them has become an eternal night. Nobel Prize recipient Eli Wiesel gives this account of his first night in Auschwitz:

Not far from us, flames, huge flames, were rising from a ditch. Something was being burned there. A truck drew close and unloaded its hold: small children. Babies! Yes, I did see this, with my own eyes...children thrown into the flames. (Is it any wonder that ever since then, sleep tends to elude me?)...I pinched myself: Was I still alive? Was I awake? How was it possible that men, women, and children were being burned and that the world kept silent?...Never shall I forget that night, the first night in camp, that turned my life into one long night seven times sealed. Never shall I forget that smoke. Never shall I forget the small faces of the children whose bodies I saw transformed into smoke under a silent sky. Never shall I forget those flames that consumed my faith forever.[1]

Blessed are the Children

The Nazis took great pleasure in burning Jewish children. Over one million children, including infants, were murdered—unblemished sacrificial lambs. It was particularly pleasurable for the Germans to burn children alive. Their screams of agony soothed their murderers and strengthened the German resolve to pull up every root of the Jewish race—no matter how small. History records other forms of genocidal frenzy toward children. After the Nazis shot the infirmed patients in the ghetto hospital of Lodz, they opened the upper story windows and threw newborn Jewish infants to their deaths. The sight of these dead infants apparently did not bring enough gratification to the hate filled hearts of the soldiers standing in the street below. Fastening their bayonets to their rifles they impaled the children before they hit the ground.[2]

After several hundred Jewish men and women were executed in the Ukrainian village of Byelaya Tserkov, their children were held for several days without food or water in a building on the outskirts

of the village. Two German military chaplains, a Protestant, Kornmann, and a Catholic divisional chaplain, Dr. Reuss, visited the
scene. Here is a portion of the report of Dr. Reuss to Lieutenant Col-
onel Groscurth, First Generalstabsoffizier, 295th Infantry Division:

*The two rooms where the children had been accommodated…were
in a filthy state. The children lay or sat on the floor which was covered
in their faeces. There were flies on the legs and abdomens of most of
the children, some of whom were only half dressed. Some of the bigger
children (two, three, four years old) were scratching the mortar from the
wall and eating it. Two men, who looked like Jews, were trying to clean
the rooms. The stench was terrible. The small children, especially those
that were only a few months old, were crying and whimpering continu-
ously….Some German soldiers who were in the courtyard told me that
they had their quarters in a house right next door and that since the afternoon of the previous day they had heard the children crying uninterrupt-
edly. Sometime during the evening of the previous day three lorry-loads of
children had already been taken away….The lorry-driver had told them
that these were children of Jew and Jewesses who had already been shot
and the children were now going to be taken to be executed. The execution
was to be carried out by Ukrainian militia. The children still in the house
were also to be shot….I asked the soldiers to make sure that nobody else,
particularly members of the local population, entered the house, in order
to avoid the conditions there being talked about further.*[3]

What is remarkable about the report by this military chaplain,
is there is no outrage over the fact that these children were about
to be executed. There is no willingness on the part of this Christian
minister to shelter these children from death. Rather, the concern
he voices to his superiors is that the condition of the children was
beginning to affect the emotions of the German soldiers. As well,
he is concerned that if the local population finds out how the children are being treated it might somehow damage the reputation of
the German military. He concludes his report with these words: "I
consider it necessary to report this matter to my HQ for two reasons:

first, there is no German watch or supervision of this house and second, German soldiers are able to enter it any time. This has indeed already happened and has provoked a reaction of indignation and criticism." [4]

It is of interest to note that this Christian military chaplain, Dr. Reuss, was ordained by the church as the Bishop of Mainz after the war ended. The Protestant chaplain, Wehrmachtoberpfarrer Kornmann F.d.R, gave a similar report of the terrible conditions. Again, his concern is not over the death sentence of these Jewish children but rather that the German soldiers were distraught over the scene: "These were Jew children whose parents had been executed. There was one group of German soldiers standing at the watch post and another standing at the corner of the house. Some of them were talking agitatedly about what they had heard and seen. As I considered it highly undesirable that such things should take place in full view of the public eye, I hereby submit this report." [5]

After receiving the reports, German military officials moved quickly to deal with the conditions of the children. The order was given to the SS to shoot the children thereby bringing the situation under control. After the war, the German officer in charge of executing these children, SS Obersturmfuhrer August Hafner, gave this testimony:

Then Blobel ordered me to have the children executed. I asked him, "By whom should the shooting be carried out?" He answered, "By the Waffen-SS." I raised an objection and said, "They are all young men. How are we going to answer to them if we make them shoot small children?" To this he said, "Then use your men." I then said, "How can they do that? They have small children as well." This tug-of-war lasted about ten minutes...I suggested that the Ukrainian militia of the Feldkommandant should shoot the children. There were no objections from either side to this suggestion....The children were taken down from the tractor. They were lined up along the top of the grave and shot so that they fell into it....They fell into the grave. The wailing was indescribable. I shall never forget the scene throughout my life. I find it very hard to bear....The ex-

ecution must have taken place in the afternoon at about 3:30 or 4:00.... Many children were hit four or five times before they died.[6]

Before the gas chambers, Nazis killed Jews with units of soldiers known as the Sonderkommandos, Einsatzgruppen, and Ordnungspolize. These groups of machine gun wielding volunteers roamed in packs like wolves. They penetrated the cities and villages of Eastern and Western Europe rounding up Jews for slaughter. Eventually, the ever-efficient Germans forced Jews to dig their own graves—and then shot them. A survivor of these killing battalions gave this account:

It was a hunt the likes of which mankind had never seen. Whole families would hide out in skrytkas as we had in Wlodzimierz, and they would be hunted down inexorably, relentlessly. Street by street, house by house, inch by inch, from attic to cellar. The Germans became expert at finding these hiding places. When they searched a house, they went tapping the walls, listening for the hollow sound that indicated a double wall. They punched holes in ceilings or floors...These were no longer limited "actions"; this was total annihilation. Teams of SS men roamed the streets, searching ditches, outhouses, bushes, barns, stables, pigsties. And they caught and killed Jews by the thousands; then by the hundreds; then by tens; and finally one by one...A former German official who served in one of these killing units gave this testimony concerning the soldiers who served with him: They "were, with a few exceptions, quite happy to take part in shootings of Jews. They had a ball!"[7]

Hermann Freidrich Graebe was a German civilian construction engineer who witnessed the murder of Jews from the Dubno Ghetto in the Ukraine. He gave this testimony, years later in the Nuremberg trial of Nazi war criminals:

During the fifteen minutes that I stood near the pit, I heard no complaint or plea for mercy. I watched a family of about 8 persons, a man and a woman, both about 50, with their children of about 1, 8 and 10, and two grown-up daughters of about 20 to 24. An old woman with snow-

white hair was holding the one-year old child in her arms and singing to it and tickling it. The child was cooing with delight. The couple was looking on with tears in their eyes. The father was holding the hand of a boy of about 10 years old and speaking to him softly; the boy was fighting his tears. The father pointed toward the sky, stroked his head, and seemed to explain something to him. At that moment the S.S. man at the pit shouted something to his comrade. The latter counted off about 20 persons and instructed them to go behind the earth mound. Among them was the family which I have mentioned. I looked for the man who did the shooting. He was an S.S. man, who sat at the edge of the narrow end of the pit, his feet dangling into the pit. He had a tommy gun on his knees and he was smoking a cigarette. The people, completely naked, went down some steps which were cut in the clay wall of the pit and clambered over the heads of the people lying there, to the place where the S.S. man directed them. They lay down in front of the dead or injured people; some caressed those who were still alive and spoke to them in low voice. Then I heard a series of shots.[8]

Willing and Ready Executioners

In his book, Hitler's Willing Executioners, Professor Daniel Jonah Goldhagen from Harvard University writes: "The Germans were cruel not only in that they incarcerated the Jews within wretched enclosures under a harsh regime designed to cause pain and suffering and then killed them in gruesome ways. Their cruelty was also personal, direct, and immediate. With their... ever-present whips and rods, with their bare hands, with their boots, the Germans pummeled Jews, lacerated their flesh, trampled them underfoot, and forced them to perform bizarre and self-abasing acts."[9]

In the history of genocide, murderers have rarely tortured and killed their victims with such demonic pleasure. Babies were torn from their mother's arms and shot point blank or thrown into burning pits. Men were made to strip naked and crawl on the ground while being beaten with clubs—then without mercy gunned down.

Who is Responsible?

Who was responsible for the Holocaust? Do we accuse Hitler? Should we hold the German nation responsible? At whose feet do we lay blame? In which direction do we point the finger of judgment and proclaim with certainty: "There is the murderous scoundrel— he did it." To do so would be uncomplicated because Hitler is an easy target. We can blame it on his anti-Semitic ideology of race. We can say that he was crazy and be done with it. We can cast the dragnet of guilt over him and move on to more relevant matters. We can avoid the massacre of the six million because it happened over sixty years ago. Many of us were not even born at the time so it has nothing to do with us. Or does it?

It is a frightening prospect to ask who was to blame for the Holocaust. This is why few ask it. The truth is that Adolph Hitler did not act alone. Who then were his accomplices? Who were the monsters who released the Zyklon B gas into the chambers of asphyxiation and death? Who were the women who served as commanders and guards in the death camps? Who were the men in the Sonderkammandos, Einsatzgruppen, and Ordnungspolizei? Were the murderers sadistic, crazed, anti-social psychopaths or just normal people who kissed their children's foreheads at night and attended church on Sunday mornings?

The larger and more pointed question is this: Had we lived in Germany during those years would we have been accomplices to the crime of genocide? Unthinkable? Yes! Unrealistic? No. The question begs an answer because history has a surreal way of repeating itself. Yes, there were individual Christian saints who acted on their own and hid Jews from the Nazis. Many of them were sent to the gas chambers themselves for their loving efforts. The Ten Boom family in the Netherlands is a wonderful example of this. They gave their lives to shelter Jewish people from murderous Nazi aggression.

A surviving daughter, Corrie, told her family's story of the daring rescue of Jews in her acclaimed book, *The Hiding Place*. Yet, for the most part, the institutional church was either ideologically aligned with Nazi anti-Semitism or neutral on the subject. Because of this, the issue of the Holocaust is the most critical issue of the church today. How could we have silently watched while our elder brothers and sisters were murdered? Will we be silent again when the present wave of anti-Semitism grows ever more violent? In his book, *The Crucifixion of the Jews*, the late Franklin H. Littell puts it this way: "The holocaust is the unfinished business of the Christian churches, the running sore unattended by its leaders and weakening to its constituents. The most important event in recent generations of church history, it is still virtually ignored in church school lessons and carefully avoided by preachers in their pulpits. More than anything else that has happened since the fourth century, it has called into question the integrity of the Christian people and confronted them with an acute identity crisis. They have not yet reestablished their right to a blessing and a name."[10]

Dr. Richard Steigmann-Gall, associate professor of history at Kent State University has recently written a fascinating book entitled *The Holy Reich*. Steigmann-Gall makes an historically accurate and detailed argument that the Nazi Third Reich saw itself as a conservative Christian movement. Here are a few thoughts from the books conclusion:

Christianity in the final analysis did not constitute a barrier to Nazism. Quite the opposite: For many of the subjects of this study, the battles waged against Germany's enemies constituted a war in the name of Christianity...Nearly all the Nazis surveyed here believed they were defending good by waging war against evil, fighting for God against the devil, for German against Jew. They were convinced that their movement did not mean the death of God, but the preservation of God. Two main currents of religious thought, each with their internal nuances and variations, existed in the Nazi movement. One of them, "positive Christian-

ity," proclaimed that Nazism was compatible with, even derived from, varieties of Christian ideology. Positive Christians suggested that Nazism was predicated on a Christian understanding of Germany's ills and their cure. In the eyes of these Nazis, the Jew was an enemy of Christianity as well as of Germany and the Aryan.[11]

Many of Hitler's speeches and writings show the conservative Christian tone of Nazism. Here is one example:

At a Christmas celebration given by the Munich branch of the NS-DAP (National Socialist German Worker's Party) in December 1926, Hitler maintained that the movement's goal was to "translate the ideals of Christ into deeds." The movement would complete "the work which Christ had begun but could not finish." On another occasion, this time behind closed doors and to fellow Nazis only, Hitler again proclaimed the centrality of Christ's teachings for this movement: "We are the first to exhume these teachings! Through us alone, and not until now, do these teachings celebrate their resurrection! Mary and Magdalene stood at the empty tomb. For they were seeking the dead man. But we intend to raise the treasures of the living Christ." In nearly evangelical tone, Hitler declares that the "true message" of Christianity is to be found only with Nazism. He claims that, where the churches failed in their mission to instill a Christian ethic in secular society, his movement would take up the task. Hitler not only read the New Testament, but professes—in private—to be inspired by it.[12]

The Crucial Issue for the Church Today

The issue of the Holocaust is crucial to the church today because of the identity of Hitler's accomplices. A nation embraced his plan for the extermination of the chosen people—willingly and enthusiastically—"The evidence that no German was ever killed or incarcerated for having refused to kill Jews is conclusive."[13] The stomach turning truth is that Germany was not a godless nation.

On the contrary, it was at the time a very powerful Christian nation. Prior to 1945 and the end of World War II Germany produced a number of the greatest theologians in the world including: Dietrich Bonhoeffer, Karl Barth, and Gerhard Kittel. From Germany came the Reformation under Martin Luther. Great hymns of our faith echoed from the depths of Germany's Christian soul—"A Mighty Fortress" and "Away in a Manger" just to mention two. Yet, anti-Semitism was not foreign to German Christians. Hatred of Jews had been proclaimed from pulpits since the Middle Ages. Hitler rose to power in part because of his hatred of the Jews. Many German Christians had been waiting for a leader to act upon their long held desire to remove the chosen from their midst: "The Nazi onslaught on the Jews was the ultimate expression of a much older hate, transmitted from generation to generation and by this time altogether unrestrained by Christian limits. But this hatred of or at best indifference to Jews was not confined to the Nazis, though it reached its extremity in them. It was endemic in the Western world. It influenced not only the perpetrators but the spectators as well..."[14]

Many Christian leaders in Germany had the same anti-Semitic leanings as Hitler. Gerard Kittel was the German theologian who edited the *Theological Dictionary of the New Testament*. His works are still standard reading for many seminary students today. Sadly though, Kittel was a committed anti-Semite. In statements made by leaders of Kittel's stature there is evidence of deep rooted genocidal thoughts within the ranks of Germany's churchmen of that period:

On June 1, 1933, the leading Protestant theologian and biblical scholar, Gerhard Kittel, gave in Tubingen a public lecture, "Die Judenfrage" ("The Jewish Problem"), which was subsequently published. The Jews, he states as a well known matter of common sense, are a racially constituted, alien body within Germany. Emancipation and assimilation, rather than rendering the Jews more fit for German society, allowed the Jews to infect the German people with their blood and spirit, with calamitous consequences. What might be the "solution" to the "Jewish Problem"? Kittel considers four. He rejects Zionism, the creation of a Jewish state in Palestine, as impractical. He rejects assimilation, because assimilation is itself a great evil which, by constitution, promotes the pollution of the racial stock. Most significantly, he explicitly considers extermination as a potential "solution": "One can try to exterminate (auszurotten) the Jews (pogroms)." Being not yet able to conceive of a state-organized systematic extermination, Kittel considers this "solution" in the light of the model of the pogrom (the violent dismantling of Jewish communities), which leads him to reject extermination as impractical, as a policy that did not and could not work. Kittel therefore settles on the eliminationist "solution" of "guest status" (Fremdlingshaft), namely the separation of Jews from their host peoples. That this eminent theologian would publicly contemplate the extermination of the Jews already in June 1933—almost in passing, without any great elaboration or justification, and as a normal, easily discussed option when trying to fashion a "solution" to the "Jewish Problem"—reveals the lethality of the… eliminationist anti-Semitism, and how ordinary its discussion must have seemed to ordinary Germans in the Germany of the early 1930's.[15]

For centuries, myths concerning Jews have flourished within the church:

There is a secret Jewish conspiracy; the Jews seek to conquer the world; Jews are an evil sect who seek to do Christians harm; Jews are by nature immoral; Jews care only for money and will do anything to get it; Jews control the press; Jews control the banks and are responsible for the economic ruination of untold numbers of Christian families; Jews are responsible for communism, Judaism commands its adherents to murder defenseless Christian children and drink their blood; Jews seek to destroy the Christian religion; Jews are unpatriotic, ever ready to sell their country out to the enemy; for the larger society to be properly protected, Jews must be segregated and their rights limited. The Church played an *important role in promulgating every one of these ideas that are central to modern anti-Semitism. Every one of them had the support of the highest Church authorities, including the popes.*[16]

The Church and the "Final Solution"

For the most part, Christian churches passionately aligned themselves to the nationalism and racism of the rising Nazi government. Without the compliance and full scale support of the church, the mass murder of six million Jews would have never happened:

The Nazi "final solution" was a logical extension of the thought of those church fathers and councils who declared God was finished with the Jewish people....Any effort to divest the churches of responsibility by categorizing the Nazis as "neopagans" ignores the centuries of false teaching which made the murder of the Jews possible and logical. Christendom was impregnated with hatred of the Jews....The wiping out of the Jews would be inconceivable without the cooperation and participation of the Christians. It came neither suddenly nor unexpectedly...It is no accident that the ideologues of Anti-Semitism have borrowed their weapons extensively from the arsenal of churchly teaching and terminology.[17]

The Teaching That Inspired It All

What was this "churchly teaching" that inspired gentile Christians to hate Jews? What kind of theology would drive Christians to separate from their Jewish spiritual fathers? What interpretation of the Scriptures could result in the murderous brutality of six million people? Actually, the church teaching that sought to separate Christians from Jews was not new to German Christianity. It began with the church fathers around the time of Justin Martyr (ca. A.D. 160):

By the time of Justin Martyr (ca. A.D. 160) a new attitude prevailed in the Church, evidenced by its appropriating the title "Israel" for itself. Until this time the Church had defined itself more in terms of continuity with the Jewish people; that is, it was an extension of Israel. There was a growing awareness, however, that the Synagogue was firm in its stance that Jesus was not the Messiah of Israel, and that on this point the Synagogue was not going to change its mind. The realization of this impasse gradually drew the Church to define itself in terms of discontinuity with—indeed, as the replacement of—Israel. To this point not only had Jewish Christians considered themselves part of the national body of Israel, but so too had Gentile believers. They saw themselves as grafted into Israel, as part of a believing remnant within Israel, not those who had usurped the place of Israel, not as a separate people independent of Israel. Therefore, as long as the Church had a reasonable balance of Jews and Gentiles in the same body, there was no tendency to take over the term Israel. But by Justin's time that balance had been lost. Though the break between Synagogue and Church had now essentially been made, the struggle between the two was far from over. A triumphalistic and arrogant Church, largely gentile in makeup, would now become more and more de-Judaized—severed from its Jewish roots. This de-judaizing developed into a history of anti-Judaism, a travesty which has extended from the second century to the present day.[18]

In his day, Justin Martyr began sowing the heretical seeds of separation. In his book, *Dialogue with Trypho, a Jew,* Justin argues that whatever used to belong to Israel has now become the property of gentile Christians. He concludes that the Gentiles are now the new Israel and the Jews are to be separated from Christians—even from God Himself. The coming church fathers would build upon this teaching. At its core, this new doctrine of the church was motivated by gentile triumphal arrogance—not Scripture. The heretical doctrine that Justin Martyr birthed later became known as Replacement Theology, Supercessionism, or Triumphalism. As we saw in chapter 1, this theology teaches that the church has replaced or superseded Israel. It teaches that Jewish people and the nation of Israel are inferior and must be replaced with something greater—The gentile Christian church.

The Warning of Jesus

Jesus warned his disciples against this very notion: "You know that the rulers of the Gentiles lord it over them, and those who are great exercise authority over them. Yet it shall not be so among you" (Matt. 20:25–26). This warning to Jewish and gentile believers alike has been for the most part rejected by Gentiles. For 1,900 years the Christian church has (for the most part) lived in arrogant triumph over her elder brothers. Paul specifically warned Gentiles in Romans 11 of the disastrous consequences of this kind of arrogant boasting:

For if the firstfruit is holy, the lump is also holy; and if the root is holy, so are the branches. And if some of the branches were broken off, and you, being a wild olive tree, were grafted in among them, and with them became a partaker of the root and fatness of the olive tree, do not boast against the branches. But if you do boast, remember that you do not support the root, but the root supports you. You will say then, "Branches were broken off that I might be grafted in." Well said. Because of unbelief they were broken off, and you stand by faith. Do not be haughty, but fear. For if God did not spare the natural branches, He may not spare you either. Therefore consider the goodness and severity of God: on those who fell, severity; but toward you, goodness. If you continue in His goodness. Otherwise you also will be cut off (Rom. 11:16–22).

For 1,900 years the Christian church has rejected Paul's warning. Have we been cut off—separated from the full expression of God's glory? For 1,900 years the church has proclaimed replacement doctrine often times with bloodthirsty frenzy. Historically, whenever the church begins to sow the seeds of anti-Semitic Replacement Theology it often leads to the murder of Jews. It also results in the "cutting off" of the church that proclaimed it. It was this arrogant doctrine of replacement that drove the church into the Dark Ages. The same teaching was behind the Crusades and the Inquisition. It was this same triumphal Replacement Theology that drove gentile baptized Christians to murder the six million. "Perhaps the most important reason the Holocaust happened is that the Church had forgotten its Jewish roots."[19]

How deeply did Replacement Theology affect the German Christians during the years of the Holocaust? Let's take a look at several key facts and allow history to testify for itself:

1. The "final solution" (the gassing and cremation of millions of Jews) was designed and implemented by Evangelical Protestant and Catholic Christians.

The Holocaust did not happen in a vacuum. Germany was a Christian nation. Many of the Nazi leaders were baptized Christians: "Kaltenbrunner, Muller, the Gestapo chief Hoess, the commandant of Auschwitz—all came from Catholic families. Himmler's godfather was a bishop of Bamberg."[20] Julius Streicher, one of Hitler's close associates, quoted Martin Luther in his defense at the Nuremberg trials. After Hitler committed suicide he was honored and commemorated for his life and work by the church. Cardinal Bertram sent out an order to the churches in his archdiocese in May 1945. He proclaimed that a solemn requiem mass be held to honor the Fuhrer "so that his and Hitler's flock could pray that the Almighty's son, Hitler, be admitted to paradise."[21] One of the last things Jews would have seen before being slaughtered was the belt buckle of the German soldier who murdered them. It read: "Gott Mit Uns" (God with us). To many, the thought of Christian men and women shooting, gassing, beating, and burning six million Jews is unthinkable and it makes us uncomfortable:

That Nazism as the world-historical metaphor for human evil and wickedness should in some way have been related to Christianity can therefore be regarded by many only as unthinkable. Christianity is not just a theological system; it is also a byword for moral and upstanding behavior of any kind. This is especially evident in the contemporary United States, where acts regarded as immoral, improper, or unethical are sanctioned as un-Christian, no matter how Christian the perpetrator or the motivation. This pedestrian usage of the phrase "Christian," no less significant for being ill defined, serves to reinforce the theological argument that the evil of Nazism surely bears no relation to the beauty and magnificence of the Christian religion in whatever form.

But men of God have been responsible for numerous acts of aggression and murder born of prejudice. The Crusades, Inquisition, and Apartheid, to name only the most obvious historical episodes, are generally regarded as "un-Christian" moments, even though it was piously Christian men who devised them and carried them through. ...By detaching Christianity from the crimes of its adherents, we create a Christianity above history, a Christianity whose teachings need not ultimately be investigated....The discovery that so many Nazis considered themselves or their movement to be Christian makes us....uncomfortable. But the very unpleasantness of this fact makes it all the more important to look it squarely in the face.[22]

2. The Holocaust was the natural result of the practice of Replacement Theology throughout church history.

Most German Christians were eager to completely sever ties with Jews. They believed that they had taken the place of Israel in the eyes of God. The problem was that Jewish people continued to prosper within the borders of Germany. How could this be? The German renaissance was largely led by Jewish artists, philosophers, and Scientists. If Christians indeed had replaced the Jews as the blessing to the world, then why were the Jews still being blessed? The majority of German Christians were so eager to eradicate themselves of the "Jewish problem" that they were willing and eager to accept fierce Nazi measures in order to exterminate them.

A Protestant publication called the Deutsche Christen declared: "In the person of the Fuhrer we behold the One sent from God, who places Germany in the presence of the Lord of History."[23] Evangelical Protestant church leaders proclaimed: "It was Hitler who had translated Christianity out of theory into unique praxis...We German Christians are the first trenchline of National Socialism...To live, fight and die for Adolph Hitler means to say Yes to the path of Christ."[24] Hitler had a long line of Christian leaders willing to stand with him to bring the final separation between Christians and Jews. An Evangelical church leadership counsel ended with this proclamation: "The unchangeable will of God meets us in the total reality of our life as it is illumined by God's revelation. It binds everyone…to the natural orders to which we are subject such as family, nation, race…In this knowledge we thank God the Lord that He has given to our people in its need a leader (Hitler) as a pious and faithful sovereign."[25]

3. Replacement Theologians used biased forms of media to indoctrinate the church.

In 1933, sixty-three percent of the German population was Protestant. Every Sunday over five million German Protestants read the Sonntagsblatter—a weekly religious newspaper. Anti-Jewish themes were common in the publication:

A survey of sixty-eight Sonntagsblatter printed between 1918 and 1933 revealed that Jews and Jewry were themes "of great topicality" in them. The press's treatment of these themes was almost invariably hostile. These religious weeklies which were devoted to the edification of their readers and to the cultivation of Christian piety, preached that the Jews were "the natural enemies of the Christian-national tradition," that they had caused "the collapse of the Christian and monarchial order," and that they were the authors of a variety of other evils…. As well, Catholic publications justified the desire to eliminate the Jewish "alien bodies" (Fremdkorper) from Germany….Before and during the Nazi period, Catholic publications…disseminated the contemporary anti-Semitic litany in ways that were often indistinguishable from the Nazis.[26]

4. The Majority of German Evangelical Protestant pastors and Catholic hierarchy held to an anti-Semitic Replacement Theology.
Listen to these statements by historians of the Holocaust:

70 to 80% of Protestant pastors had allied themselves with the anti-Semitic German National People's Party.[27]
As Jewish children were being driven from the nation's schools,

Jewish scientists from the nation's scientific organizations, Jewish government employees and teachers from their jobs, the message was clear: The Church had no objection.[28]

Adolph Hitler waited until 1941. And when he saw that no one wanted the Jews and no major power was prepared to pay ransom, he struck.[29]

It is…no surprise that although the Catholic bishops did make a few public statements that decried the treatment or killing of foreigners, they did not speak out explicitly against the extermination of the Jews (of which they had full knowledge)…Never once did any German bishop, Catholic or Protestant, speak out publicly on behalf of the Jews…they forsook the Jews of Germany utterly, in this sense, the religious leaders of Germany were men of God second and Germans first—so powerful was the anti-Semitic model—for these German men of God could not bring themselves to utter that Jews "are part of the human race" and to declare to their flocks that the moral laws were not suspended for the treatment of Jews…. It was not the anti-Semites who were the exceptions among the Christian leadership in Germany. The rarities were those who remained untouched by anti-Semitism.[30]

5. German Christian leaders successfully influenced a nation to believe that murdering Jews was permitted by God:

After the war was over, a German Protestant theologian, Martin Niemoller, gave a lecture in Zurich in 1946. Here is a portion of his testimony: "Christianity in Germany bears a greater responsibility before God than the National Socialists, the S.S. and the Gestapo. We ought to have recognized the Lord Jesus in the brother who suffered and was persecuted despite him being a communist or a Jew… Are not we Christians much more to blame, am I not much more guilty, than many who bathed their hands in blood?"[31]

The Holocaust was a great apostasy that the church endorsed: "The time of testing ended in death for six million Jews and apostasy by uncounted millions of Christians. The critical factor was the same in both cases: peoplehood. The Jews died because they were standing alone and not numbered among the nations of the earth. The Christians, with the exception of a minority of martyrs and confessors, betrayed the life into which they were called."[32]

6. The natural result of Replacement Theology is violence toward Jews.

Father Wilhelm Schmidt was a churchman who embraced the National Socialism of the Nazi Party. Here is what he had to say: "Down the ages war was always for the Jews merely good business, while for the Aryans it meant a terrible loss of blood...No honest man can any longer deny that Judaism wants to destroy us. To help ensure that this does not happen is the task and duty of every German, Christian and Aryan today."[33]

Bishop Martin Sasse of Thuringia celebrated Martin Luther's birthday with these words: "On November 10, 1938, on Luther's birthday, the synagogues are burning in Germany. The German people, he urged, ought to heed these words 'of the greatest anti-Semite of his time, the warner of his people against the Jews.'"[34]

Goldhagen tells us that during the Holocaust: "In the ranks of the clergy at all levels, numerous voices could be heard vilifying the Jews in Nazi-like terms, hurling imprecations at them, and acclaiming their persecution at the hands of their country's government. No serious historian would dispute the anti-Nazi theologian Karl Barth's verdict contained in his parting letter before leaving Germany in 1935: 'For the millions that suffer unjustly, the Confessing Church does not yet have a heart.'"[35]

7. German Christians did not believe it to be morally wrong to exterminate Jews.

Adolph Eichmann was the SS leader who implemented the "final solution." Eichmann was a Protestant who grew up attending Bible classes at the YMCA. During his trial in Jerusalem Eichmann gave this defense: "I am not guilty of shedding blood." He was simply going along with the "sound sense of the people."[36] German Evangelical Protestants believed that exterminating Jews in the gas chambers was actually the most humane way of dealing with the "Jewish problem." They called this policy of murder "humane extermination."[37]

8. German Christians were so committed to the tenants of Replacement Theology that they separated themselves even from Jews who had converted to Christianity:

At the Evangelical Church one must level the grave reproach that it did not stop the persecution of the children of her faith (the baptized Jews)—indeed that from the pulpits she implored (God's) blessing for the work of those who worked against the children of her faith—and at the majority of the Evangelical faithful the reproach must be leveled that they consciously waged this struggle against their own brothers in faith—and that both church and church members drove away from their community, from their churches people with whom they were united in worship, as one drives away mangy dogs from one's door.[38]

For 1,900 years the church has for the most part been living in a long endless night. After centuries of boasting against the Jewish people we have separated ourselves from the nourishing sap of the olive tree—our Jewish heritage. However, a light is dawning upon a remnant of gentile believers who are willing to end the separation and begin the search for their roots. Part of our journey back will include facing the truth of what we have done to our Jewish elder brothers and sisters. Only when we learn from history can we avoid repeating it again. If one tries to run from history, history will eventually catch up with him. In our next chapter we will discover the origin of the yellow Star of David the Jews were forced to wear during the Holocaust. The star was used to separate Jews from the surrounding Christian society. The answer will surprise you.

The Yellow Patch

*It was Judaism that brought the concept of a
God-given universal moral law into the world
....the Jew carries the burden of God in history
(and) for this has never been forgiven.*
The Reverend Edward H. Flannery
National Conference of Catholic Bishops

*We realize now that many, many centuries of blindness
have dimmed our eyes, so that we no longer see the
beauty of Thy Chosen People and no longer recognize
in their faces the features of our firstborn brother.
We realize that our brows are branded with the mark of
Cain. Centuries long has Abel lain in blood and tears,
because we had forgotten thy love. Forgive us the curse
which we unjustly laid on the name of the Jews. Forgive
us that with our curse, we crucified Thee a second time.*
A prayer composed by Pope John XXIII
shortly before his death.

You have probably seen the pictures—Jewish men, women, and children being led to the gas chambers like lambs to the slaughter. If you look closely at the photographs, you will see that every Jew has a distinguishing mark sewn on their clothing or worn as an arm band. To separate Jews from Christian Gentiles, the Germans required all Jews to wear a patch. The patch was a Star of David with the word "Jude" (German for Jew) written on it. The star was yellow in color. But, of course, we do not know this because the pictures we have of the star are not in color. Maybe it is appropriate that the yellow Star of David could only be photographed in black and white. The contrast of light and shadow, grey and white—hues of contrasting shades, tell the story of why the patch was created: contrast and separation. The Germans were masters at separating the strong from the weak, desirables from undesirables and the healthy from the sick.

A Yellow Patch of Separation

Who was the Nazi mastermind that came up with the concept of using a yellow patch for segregation? The fact is that the Nazis rarely had an original idea. The history of segregating Jews with yellow patches started long before Hitler's Third Reich and the "final solution." We get an idea where the patch came from in this order given by the Nazis in 1939: "We are returning to the Middle Ages. The yellow patch once again becomes a part of Jewish dress. Today an order was announced that all Jews, no matter what age or sex, have to wear a band of 'Jewish yellow,' 10 centimeters wide, on their right arm, just below the armpit."[1]

If the Nazi order of 1939 was simply reinstituting a racial law of Jewish segregation from the Middle Ages, then by whose order was this anti-Semitic law originally established? The fact is that the yellow patch came into being during the fourth Lateran Council in the year 1215. The sixty-eighth canonical law established by the church in this council states: "In some provinces a difference in dress distinguishes the Jews or Saracens from the Christians, but in certain others such a confusion has grown up that they cannot be distinguished by any difference....we decree that such Jews and Saracens of both sexes in every Christian province and at all times shall be marked off in the eyes of the public from other peoples through the character of their dress."

That a Christian pope would establish a worldwide policy of segregating Jews from Christians is shocking. However, if you take into account the fierce hatred and prejudice that had been brewing in Christians towards Jews for centuries, it makes the decision of Pope Innocent III to create the yellow patch clear. The church had a long history of murderous violence toward Jews well before the yellow patch was used by the Nazis. Consider the Crusades and the Inquisition.

A Resurrection Awaits Us

You might be asking: "Why is it necessary to know the gritty details of the church's (both Catholic and Protestant) historic mistreatment of the Jewish people?" The reason is because in relation to the Jew, American Christianity is at a crossroads today. If we refuse to choose the path of self discovery—painful as it is—and overlook the fact that for the last 1,900 years our collective hands have been stained with Jewish blood, then it is inevitable that we will fall prey to the same anti-Semitism that has plundered the European church. As we will see in our next chapter, if we don't learn from history then history is bound to repeat itself.

The church has never recovered from its collaboration with the Nazis in the "final solution." Wonderfully, in some corners of the church, including the Catholic Church, there has been an admission of guilt for the Holocaust. But, a full scale repentance has yet to occur within a broad expression of Christianity. The continual avoidance of our past is keeping us from our destiny. The Holocaust was a self-inflicted mortal blow to the church. Amazingly, the Jews recovered and experienced a resurrection from the ashes of the gas chambers in the return to their Promised Land—Israel. A future spiritual resurrection awaits them when they embrace their Messiah, Jesus. A resurrection of life and wholeness awaits the church as well. The first glimpse of hope will arise when we acknowledge the sins in our collective history.

The call of the church in this hour is to define once and for all our relationship to the Jewish people—both Messianic Jews (those who have accepted Jesus as their Messiah—of which there are several hundred thousand) and the world Jewish community (which for the most part has not come to faith in Jesus as Messiah). A dynamic way to discover this is to find out why the relationship was broken in the first place and then to examine the history of the separation— now encompassing 1,900 years. If we don't get it right on this one, we face a perilous future. The two minute warning alarm has sounded. The Jewish Messiah Jesus is sending a revolution of separation to the earth in this hour. Growing ever more hateful towards the Jewish people, Satan is planning another holocaust. Anti-Semitic rumblings deep within the core of Christianity are beginning to spew hot molten lava over her sides—again. Yet Jesus is still interceding in heaven for the healing of this divide.

A Great Coming Revolution of Separation

Jesus describes a great separation that will occur at the end of the age. One day the nations will be separated from the Lord based on their harsh treatment of His brethren. A righteous remnant of gentile believers will be drawn to the Lord as well, based on their kind treatment of His brethren. The scene of this epic coming revolution of separation is described by the Lord in Matthew 25:

When the Son of Man comes in His glory, and all the holy angels with Him, then He will sit on the throne of His glory. All the nations will be gathered before Him, and He will separate them one from another, as a shepherd divides his sheep from the goats. And He will set the sheep on

His right hand, but the goats on the left. Then the King will say to those on His right hand, "Come, you blessed of My Father, inherit the kingdom prepared for you from the foundation of the world: for I was hungry and you gave Me food. I was thirsty and you gave Me drink. I was a stranger and you took Me in. I was naked and you clothed Me. I was sick and you visited Me; I was in prison and you came to Me." Then the righteous will answer Him, saying, "Lord, when did we see You hungry and feed You, or thirsty and give You drink? When did we see You a stranger and take You in, or naked and clothe You? Or when did we see You sick, or in prison, and come to you?" And the King will answer and say to them, "Assuredly, I say to you, inasmuch as you did it to one of the least of these My brethren, you did it to Me." Then He will also say to those on the left hand, "Depart from Me, you cursed, into the everlasting fire prepared for the devil and his angels: for I was hungry and you gave Me no food; I was thirsty and you gave Me no drink; I was a stranger and you did not take Me in, naked and you did not clothe Me, sick and in prison and you did not visit Me." Then they also will answer Him, saying, "Lord, when did we see You hungry or thirsty or a stranger or naked or sick or in prison, and did not minister to You?" Then He will answer them, saying, "Assuredly, I say to you, inasmuch as you did not do it to one of the least of these, you did not do it to Me." And these will go away into everlasting punishment, but the righteous into eternal life (Matt. 25:31–46).

This scene describes the judgment of the gentile nations that have historically persecuted the Jewish people—the "brethren" of the Lord. Notice verse 40: "Inasmuch as you did it to one of the least of these My brethren, you did it to Me." Jesus is Jewish, and when He came to earth the first time "He came to His own" (John 1:11), the Jewish people. When Jesus speaks of His "brethren" in the context of Matthew 25, He is speaking of the Jewish people. When He returns the second time He will judge the nations for how they have treated the Jews. In this passage in Matthew 25, Jesus is affirming what the prophet Joel proclaimed concerning the judgment of the nations based on their dealings with the people of

Israel: "For behold, in those days and at that time, when I bring back the captives of Judah and Jerusalem, I will also gather all nations, and bring them down to the Valley of Jehoshaphat; and I will enter into judgment with them there On ACCOUNT OF MY PEOPLE, MY HERITAGE ISRAEL, whom they have scattered among the nations; they have also divided up My land" (Joel 3:1–2).

Jesus is drawing a line of demarcation between those who love Israel and those who hate her. From this divine separation a remnant of righteous Gentiles will arise that will embrace their long forgotten Jewish elder brothers and sisters. Paul the Apostle speaks about this spiritual resurrection of gentile believers in the last days. When Jews are restored to their Messiah Paul says that a resurrection will occur: "Now if their [Jews] fall is riches for the world and their failure riches for the Gentiles, how much more their fullness!... For if their being cast away is the reconciling of the world, what will their acceptance be but life from the dead?" (Rom. 11:12, 15).

Our True Identity

Be at peace and take courage. A resurrection is coming to the true body of Christ. Our Messiah Jesus is bringing us into our true identity. He is restoring to us that which has been lost over the last 1,900 years of wandering away from our foundation. He is returning us to our roots in this hour. A full restoration awaits us and it will be like life from the dead.

Be assured—the journey we are about to take in this chapter is a painful one. However, it will be impossible to have any hope of wholeness in our faith until we come to the recognition that centuries of Jewish hatred has left Christianity a mere reflection of what it was meant to be—what it should be—what it can be. The rejection of our nourishing root system has metamorphosed us into a disjointed body. God's Word to Abraham was that through him all the families of the earth would be blessed (Gen. 12:3). We must ask ourselves: why are Christian families fracturing at an alarming rate? Why are people who were raised in church leaving the faith in unprecedented numbers? The Jews are known as the people of the Book. For thousands of years they have preserved the covenants and the promises. Why has the gentile church in many quarters rejected the infallibility and inerrancy of Scripture?

Something is desperately wrong. It seems like a dam has broken and we cannot stop the hemorrhaging. On the outside it appears that all is well. Christians seem happy. But something is desperately missing. Could it be that we have lost our way? Could it be that we have moved the ancient boundary stones and rejected the ancient paths? Remember, true loyalty to God is to hear and obey His Word in the power of the Holy Spirit. This is not an hour to avoid truth but to embrace it—even if it's painful. Somehow, we must find our way back to the place where the relationship with our Jewish spiritual fathers was severed and heal the divide.

After the birth of the church, the Jewish apostles opened the door to the Gentiles who desired to become part of the commonwealth of Israel. Graciously, these early Jewish elders of our faith chose not to place a heavy load of spiritual requirements on their new believing gentile brothers and sisters. Up until this time, Jews and Gentiles who had come to faith in Jesus worshipped together in the synagogue. Gentiles did not see their faith as being separate from the faith of Jews, but a continuation of God's eternal covenant with Israel. These Jewish and gentile people who had come to faith in Jesus saw themselves as "one new man" in Jesus. Paul the Jewish apostle talks about this one new man in Ephesians 2:11–16:

Therefore remember that you, once Gentiles in the flesh—who are called Uncircumcision by what is called the Circumcision made in the flesh by hands—that at that time you were without Christ, being aliens from the commonwealth of Israel and strangers from the covenants of promise, having no hope and without God in the world. But now in Christ Jesus you who once were far off have been brought near by the blood of Christ. For He Himself is our peace, who has made both one and has broken down the middle wall of separation, having abolished in His flesh the enmity, that is, the law of commandments contained in ordinances, so as to create in Himself one new man from the two thus making peace, and that He might reconcile them both to God in one body through the cross, thereby putting to death the enmity.

Jewish and gentile believers in the early church worshiped together as "one new man." Gentiles came under the teaching and covering of their Jewish spiritual fathers. Although Jewish believers retained their own identity and continued in their unique expression of faith in their Jewish Messiah, they did not force these practices upon the newly saved Gentiles. They graciously proclaimed to Gentiles that they were now fellow citizens with Jewish saints, members of the household of God, part of the commonwealth of Israel and fellow heirs of all of the covenantal blessings of Abraham. Thus, gentile believers saw themselves as grafted into Israel, as part of a believing remnant within Israel, not as a people who had usurped the place of Israel, or become independent or separate from Israel.

Early Jewish apostles, realizing God's kingdom purpose in the salvation of the Gentiles, said these words upon hearing the report of the salvation of Cornelius—a Gentile who had received Jesus: "When they heard these things they became silent; and they glorified God, saying, 'Then God has also granted to the Gentiles repentance to life.'" (Acts 11:18).

As the persecution and dispersion of Jews from Israel increased under the heavy hand of the Roman Empire, gentile Christians began to outnumber Jewish believers in Jesus. Gradually, Gentiles rejected the Hebraic apostolic foundation in which the church was built. Towards the middle of the second century there came a full parting of the relationship between Jewish and gentile people of the Way. The "one new man" became two separate groups. In complete rebellion towards their spiritual Jewish elder brothers, gentile church leaders taught renegade arrogant principles that defied the very foundation of who they were as covenantal members of the spiritual commonwealth of Israel. They erroneously proclaimed that the gentile church had now surpassed the Jewish chosen people. The church began to define itself in terms of discontinuity with and replacement of Israel. They arrogantly proclaimed that God had broken His covenant with Israel because of Israel's sins. They said gentile Christians were now the new Israel and that Jews were sons of the devil worthy of severe punishment. They taught that the gentile church had now replaced and superseded Israel. Severed from its Jewish foundation and roots, gentile Christianity began a wilderness journey that still continues. In arrogant pride, gentile Christians boasted against the Jewish branches and failed to heed Paul's warning to gentile Christians in Romans 11: "And if some of the branches were broken off, and you, being a wild olive tree, were grafted in among them, and with them became a partaker of the root and fatness of the olive tree, do not boast against the branches. But if you do boast, remember that you do not support the root, but the root supports you" (Rom. 11:17–18).

A Scarlet Thread

In this chapter we will unveil a thread that has been sewn throughout church history. This thread is the continual dehumanization, segregation, and murder of the Jewish people by baptized Christians. We will show that the church has historically sponsored anti-Semitism either through false teaching or through instituting racial laws of segregation. Historically, both have led to violence and murder. In fact, there has never been a time in the church's history when it has been silent in its attempt to distinguish itself apart from and above the Jewish people—either through bad teaching or bad behavior.

In coming chapters we will unveil the sobering truth that this blood stained scarlet thread has not been broken. It continues to weave through Christian seminaries and pulpits of America. How we respond to this ongoing Christian hatred of Jewish people is the most important question facing the body of Christ today.

Many church historians avoid the horror of this long standing hatred. The milestones in the church's systematic dehumanization of the chosen people have been buried along the way. As a result, much of the information you are about to read might be new to you. It is difficult to learn from the mistakes of our collective past if they are erased. If we fail to see that the church doctrine that inspired the violent acts of mass murder of the Jews is still a widely accepted teaching of the modern church, how can we look ourselves in the mirror and feel no sense of moral obligation to cut the scarlet thread that ties us to the blood stained past?

Identificational Repentance is Necessary

Our generation is responsible to break the awful cycle of Jewish hatred in our time. We are responsible to connect the historical dots so that we know what to beware of today. Again, those who don't learn from history are bound to repeat it. The church can never heal her gaping wound until she faces the sins of her past—in the case of the Holocaust, a very recent past. Because our future glory depends on our care and concern for the Jewish brethren of the Jewish Messiah, Jesus, history demands our present willingness to see the past in its full reality—without covering its shame. The only hope of future glory is a righteous remnant of gentile believers who are willing to boldly confront the past in all of its ugliness. If you made it through the previous chapter on the Holocaust without putting this book down in gasping rage at its conclusions, then you most likely are the willing brave heart ready to stand in identificational repentance for the church's blood stained hands. Because we are part of the church, we have a right and a responsibility to repent for our collective sins. We have buried this historical hatred for too long. It's time for a remnant of gentile Christians to take responsibility, repent for the 1,900 years of jealousy that led to the persecution and murder of our elder brothers, and heal the divide. Yes, there are wonderful stories of heroic gentile saints who over the centuries of time have defended and sheltered Jews in their suffering. Some of these stories are recorded in upcoming chapters. First however, it's important that we face the burden of our past. Hannah Arendt said: "Comprehension does not mean denying the outrageous, deducing the unprecedented from precedents, or explaining phenomena by such analogies and generalities that the impact of reality and the shock of experience are no longer felt. It means, rather, examining and bearing consciously the burden which our century has placed on us—neither denying its existence nor submitting weakly to its weight."[2]

It would be impossible to condense 1,900 years of Christian violence toward Jews into one chapter. We will briefly look at three areas: church fathers, church superstitions, and church racial laws.

Church Fathers

When it comes to church fathers, the history books rightly honor them. It is no doubt their study of the Word of God helped shape the church in its mission and practice. Great fruit has come from many of the doctrinal foundations they built in the Christian faith. We should give honor where honor is due, and we are grateful for much of their work in laying theological foundations of doctrine and reformation. However, several church fathers and early leaders pursued the doctrine of the replacement of Israel by the church. This erroneous teaching has resulted in the persecution of Jews by Christians over the centuries. Here are just a few examples:

Justin Martyr. In his Dialogue, Justin emphasized that the principles of Scripture that once belonged to Jews were now owned solely by Gentiles—they "are not yours but ours...We too, would observe your circumcision of the flesh, your Sabbath days, and in a word, all of your festivals, if we were not aware of the reason why they were imposed upon you, namely, because of your sins and the hardness of heart."[3]

53

John Chrysostom. John Chrysostom was known as the "Golden Mouthed." He was a very eloquent orator but sadly he often used his skill to speak against Jews:

There is no sneer too mean, no gibe too bitter for him to fling at the Jewish people. No text is too remote to be able to be twisted to their confusion, no argument is too casuistical, no blaspheme too startling for him to employ...On the strength of Psalm 106:37, he states that they "sacrificed their sons and daughters to devils": they outraged nature; and overthrew from their foundations the laws of relationship. They are become worse than the wild beasts, and for no reason at all, with their own hands they murder their own offspring, to worship the avenging devils who are the foes of our life...The synagogues of the Jews are the homes of idolatry and devils, even though they have no images in them. They are worse even than heathen circuses...I hate the Jews for they have the law and they insult it.[4]

St. Augustine. Though more temperate toward Jews than other church fathers, Augustine was responsible for much of the groundwork of Replacement Theology. A major building block in his doctrinal stance about the Jews was his tragic misinterpretation of Psalm 59:11 in his work: The City of God: "Do not slay them, lest my people forget; Scatter them by Your power, and bring them down, O Lord Our shield." Here is how Augustine interprets this passage: "Therefore God has shown the Church in her enemies the Jews the grace of His compassion, since, as saith the apostle, 'their offence is the salvation of the Gentiles.' And therefore He has not slain them, that is, He has not let the knowledge that they are Jews be lost in them, although they have been conquered by the Romans, lest they should forget the law of God....But it was not enough that he (God) should say, 'Slay them not, lest they should at last forget Thy law,' unless he had also added, 'Disperse them.'"[5]

In his book, *Future Israel*, Dr. Barry Horner comments on Augustine's view of Psalm 59:11: "So by way of imposition upon the text, David's enemies are interpreted as the Jews, being enemies of the church....Consequently, the Augustinian legacy kept the Jews dispersed, disgraced, and depressed—except for the hope of their individual conversion, or until their national conversion at the end of this age when they would then become absorbed into the one true, holy, catholic, apostolic church."[6]

Augustine taught that Israel was like Esau who gave up his birthright to his younger brother Jacob (called Israel) who, according to Augustine, represented the gentile church. Based on this idea, Augustine believed it was now the right of the church to call themselves Israel because they had replaced Israel: "For if we hold with a firm heart the grace of God which hath been given us, we are Israel, the seed of Abraham...Let therefore no Christian consider himself alien to the name of Israel...The Christian people then is rather Israel...But that multitude of Jews, which was deservedly reprobated for its perfidy, for the pleasures of the flesh sold their birthright, so that they belonged not to Jacob, but rather to Esau."[7]

Peter the Venerable. "Yes, you Jews. I say, do I address you; you, who till this very day, deny the Son of God. How long, poor wretches, will ye not believe the truth? Truly I doubt whether a Jew can be really human....I lead out from its den a monstrous animal, and show it as a laughing stock in the amphitheater of the world, in the sight of all people. I bring thee forward, thou Jew, thou brute beast, in the sight of all men." [8]

Martin Luther. His ideas concerning the Jews were quoted in Adolph Hitler's book, *Mein Kampf*, as a basis of support for his antagonism toward them. Again, we should honor Martin Luther for his work in reforming the church, yet this should not prevent us from facing the truth of what he taught concerning Jewish people:

What shall we Christians do with this damned, rejected race of Jews? Since they live among us and we know about their lying and blasphemy and cursing, we can not tolerate them if we do not wish to share in their lies, curses, and blasphemy. In this way we cannot quench the inextinguishable fire of divine rage nor convert the Jews. We must prayerfully and reverentially practice a merciful severity...First, their synagogues should be set on fire, and whatever does not burn up should be covered over spread over with dirt so that no one may ever be able to see a cinder or stone of it. And this ought to be done for the name of God and of Christianity in order that God may see that we are Christians, and that we have not wittingly tolerated or approved of such public lying, cursing, and blaspheming of His Son and His Christians.

Secondly, their homes should likewise be broken down and destroyed. For they perpetrate the same things there that they do in their synagogues. For this reason they ought to be put under one roof or in a stable, like gypsies....

Thirdly, they should be deprived of their prayer books and Talmuds in which such idolatry, lies, cursing, and blasphemy are taught.

Fourthly, their rabbis must be forbidden under threat of death to teach any more...To sum up, dear princes and nobles who have Jews in your domains, if this advice of mine does not suit you, then find a better one so that you and we may all be free of this insufferable devilish burden—the Jews.

Even if they were punished in the most gruesome manner that the streets ran with their blood, that their dead would be counted, not in the hundred thousands, but in the millions, still they must insist on being right even if after these 1,500 years they were in misery another 1,500 years, still God must be a liar and they must be correct. In sum, they are the devil's children, damned to hell...[9]

Church Superstitions

The Desecration of the Host. In 1215 the Fourth Lateran Council of the church established the doctrine of transubstantiation. This is the teaching that the wafer and wine served in Holy Communion or Eucharist actually becomes the body and blood of the Lord. A long standing myth would arise from this new doctrine that would cause the murder of large numbers of Jews. It was a common practice for Christian women to be employed by Jewish families as nursemaids for their infant children. If she received the host on the Lord's day and then nursed a Jewish infant on Monday, then the actual body of Jesus would be transferred from her stomach into her milk and then proceed into the mouth of a Jewish baby. In effect, the Jewish baby would be eating the body of Christ and therefore crucifying the Son of God all over again. In his book, The Devil and the Jews, Joshua Trachtenberg states: "This notion prevailed for several hundred years and received repeated official support; as late as 1581 Gregory XIII, in his bull Antiqua Judaeorum, sanctioned it anew as sufficient reason for forbidding the employment of Christian nurses by Jews."[10]

This myth would eventually metamorphose into darker tales of Jewish complicity in bringing harm to the actual body of Christ. Christians were believed to be coaxed and bribed by Jews to retain the wafer after mass and deliver it into their hands. Upon having the host in possession, the Jew (according to this myth) would stab it through with nails—crucifying it—until the actual blood of Jesus flowed from the wafer. This lie was proclaimed from church pulpits across Europe and inspired murderous bands of Christians to hunt down Jews for public execution.

When a Jew was suspected by the church of mutilating the host, the entire Jewish community suffered along with the individual. The belief was that the Jews corporately crucified the host during their feasts and sometimes even at wedding ceremonies. In 1267 an order came from the Council of Vienna requiring all Jews to return to their homes whenever they heard the sounding of the bell that signified a host was being carried through the streets in a church procession. They did not want those who were bent on crucifying Christ a second time coming close to His body. In their book, Why the Jews?, Dennis Prager and Joseph Telushkin describe how the myth of host desecration,

....led to the torture and murder of thousands of Jews...In 1243, only twenty-eight years after the Fourth Lateran Council, the first accusation of "host desecration" occurred in Berlitz, near Berlin. The city's entire Jewish community was burned alive for allegedly torturing a wafer. Charges of "host desecration" spread throughout Europe. In Prague, in 1389, the Jewish community was collectively accused of attacking a monk carrying a *wafer. Large mobs of Christians surrounded the Jewish neighborhood and offered the Jews the choice of baptism or death. Refusing to be baptized, three thousand Jews were murdered. In Berlin, in 1510, twenty-six Jews were burned and two beheaded for reportedly "desecrating the host." A charge of host desecration was reported as late as 1836 in Romania.*[11]

It is interesting to note that the same church council that established the doctrine of transubstantiation (Fourth Lateran in 1215) also decreed the law of the yellow patch required to be worn on the clothing of every Jew. Was this a way to prevent Jews from slipping into church mass unaware in order to steal the body of Christ?

The Devil Incarnate. The church taught that the Jew was not actually human. Trachtenberg states:

The Jew was not human—not in the sense that the Christian was. He was a creature of an altogether different nature, of whom normal human reactions could not be expected....What then? He was the devil's creature! Not a human being but a demonic, a diabolic beast fighting the forces of truth and salvation with Satan's weapons, was the Jew as medieval Europe saw him....against such a foe no well of hatred was too deep, no war of extermination effective enough until the world was rid of his menace...The two inexorable enemies of Jesus, then, in Christian legend were the devil and the Jew.[12]

The church used a passage from the Old Testament to verify that Jews were actually satanic beings. Exodus 34:29 says, "Now it was so, when Moses came down from Mount Sinai (and the two tablets of the Testimony were in Moses' hand when he came down from the mountain), that Moses did not know that the skin of his face shone while he talked with Him." After being in the presence of God, the face of Moses illuminated beams of light. However, the text endorsed by the church (Aquila and the vulgate) read: "His face had horns." The artist Michelangelo fell prey to this misinterpretation of Scripture when he painted his famous "Moses" with two horns protruding from his brow. Eventually, Jews in Europe were forced to wear a distinguishing horn somewhere on their clothing. After the Vienna Council of 1267, Jews were required to wear a horned hat. Jews in France were ordered by law to attach a horn to the yellow Star of David patch already on their outer clothing.

The Blood Libel. This myth is the most harrowing of all and is responsible for vast numbers of Jewish murders at the hands of professing, baptized Christians. According to this belief, Jews drank the blood of Christian martyrs during the feast of Passover. The Christian clergy went to great lengths to spread this superstition to the masses. Sermons about the horrors suffered by blood drained Christians—often children—were common. You can only imagine the revenge born in the hearts of the gullible medieval populace who accepted this myth as fact. Here are a few of the many accusations of the blood libel:

1234, Lauda a.d. Tauber: Jews accused of murder of Christian child—the first such accusation in Germany

1235, Fulda: On Christmas day, while their parents are at church, five boys killed and their blood collected in bags smeared with wax

1267, Pforzheim: On July 1, child killed and his blood collected on folded pieces of linen

1270, Weissenburg: Jews accused of suspending child by the feet, on June 29, and opening every artery in his body in order to obtain all his blood

1285, Munich: In October, Jews accused of kidnapping a child

1286, Oberwesel: "The good Werner" slowly tortured to death by Jews for three days

1287, Berne: A boy, Rudolph, tortured, and his head finally cut off

1293, Krems: Jews kill a boy "in order to get his blood"[13]

The belief in the blood libel didn't end in the Middle Ages. An account as late as 1840 is an indication of how deeply this myth has persisted. An Italian monk—Father Tommaso—residing in Damascus, Syria was last seen heading in the direction of the Jewish quarter of the city. He was never to return to his monastery. Word spread that he had been murdered by the Jews so that his blood could be drained for Passover. The church launched an immediate aggressive investigation and interrogation of Jewish suspects. A local rabbi was accused of instigating the murder. Here is an account of the rabbi's torture:

On March 1st, the rabbi recalled, he had been brought in for questioning by the pasha, who ordered him to produce the bottle of the friar's blood that one of the other tortured Jews had claimed he had. When the rabbi said that no such bottle existed, the pasha threatened to cut his head off, and then had him thrown into a pool of frigid water. Each time he bobbed up to breathe, the soldiers clubbed him on the head. When the rabbi was finally pulled out, he was flogged until he fainted, then flogged again until he once more passed out. The interrogators paused to offer him a way out. If he would confess, he would not only be granted a pardon, but a life pension as well. When he refused, they placed a tourniquet around his forehead, and ratcheted it so tightly that twice the rope broke. Subsequently they dragged him by a rope tied to his penis and crushed his genitals. Unlike most of the other Jews subjected to these methods, the rabbi stood by his story.[14]

It was reported by a Jewish shop owner whose store was nearby the city gate that he witnessed the friar and his servant leaving the city at dusk. Muslim residents who lived near the store gave public testimony that the Jew was telling the absolute truth. The reward of the shop owner's testimony was that he was clubbed to death. The blood libel myth is widely held in the Muslim world to this day.

Forced Baptisms. Because of the church's racial laws, Jews were forcibly locked into ghettos in Rome resulting in a life of poverty. The only way out of the ghetto was to convert to Christianity through baptism. Often, young Jewish men wanting a better life, would make their way (usually by night) to the House of the Catechumens. This was an institute designed by the church for the conversion of Jews. In his book, *The Popes Against the Jews*, Brown University professor David I. Kertzer writes: "The Ghetto and the House of the Catechumens were the two cornerstones of the Church's Jewish policy. The ghetto embodied all the restrictions that the popes believed had to be placed on the Jews, while the Catechumens was the place designed to save them, the portal through which Jews could escape the ghetto and enter into normal, Christian society."[15] The House of the Catechumens did not offer any more freedom than the ghetto. If a new convert was discovered outside after sundown they would be arrested by the papal police and be subjected to a month's stay in the dungeon chained to a wall and fed bread and water. Those who chose to leave the ghetto for the House of the Catechumens were desperately poor and hungry. The rector of Rome's Catechumens for thirty-seven years, Francesco Rovira Bonet, gave this report of the condition of the Jews when they came for "conversion": "Those who come to the House of the Catechumens to embrace the holy faith, come there wearing filthy rags.... and are so disgusting that it gives one chills to see them."[16]

Upon entering the house, a Jew was required to sign a covenant to convert and then ordered to list the names of his wife and children. With signed agreement in hand, church authorities led by papal police entered the ghetto and kidnapped the family of the convert by force. Jeremiah and Pazienza Anticoli were parents of a young son named Lazzaro. They lived in the Jewish ghetto in Rome in the year 1815. Jeremiah desired a better life away from the grim realities of his surroundings and so ventured into the catechumen and proclaimed his desire to convert. He was told by the rector that he must prove his sincerity by offering his wife and son to the church. Pazienza and Lazzaro were then extracted from the ghetto. For the next six weeks Pazienza, only nineteen years old, was held captive by the church as a procession of priests and nuns tried to convince her to convert. After thirty-nine days Pazienza had not converted. She argued that she was born a Jew, and she would die a Jew. All she wanted was to go home with her son. Pazienza did go home, and, on January 11, 1816, eight days later, Jeremiah—after realizing that he would be separated from his wife forever—returned to the ghetto as well. And what of the little boy Lazzaro? He was baptized by the church as a Christian and given a new name: "Bernardo Maria Fortunato Andrea Cardeli."[17] His parents—Jeremiah and Pazienza would never see him again.

Church Racial Laws

We stated earlier that the Nazis simply built upon the foundation of anti-Semitism the church had been building throughout her history. Without the support of the church—both Protestant and Catholic, the Holocaust would never have happened. In his book, *The Destruction of the European Jews*, Raul Hilberg connects the Nazi policies toward Jews to the medieval canonical laws of the church. These laws had been enforced and carried out towards European Jews for hundreds of years. The Nazis simply reinforced the legal precedent already established by the church.

CANONICAL LAW	NAZI MEASURE
• Prohibition of intermarriage and of sexual intercourse between Christians and Jews, Synod of Elvira, 306	• Law for the Protection of German Blood and Honor, September 15, 1935 (RGB1 I, 1146)
• Jews and Christians not permitted to eat together, Synod of Elvira, 306	• Jews barred from dining cars (Transport Minister to Interior Minister, December 30, 1939, Document NG–3995)
• Jews not allowed to hold public office, Synod of Clermot, 535	• Law for the Re-establishment of the Professional Civil Service, April 7, 1933 (RGB1 I, 175)
• Jews not allowed to employ Christian servants or possess Christian slaves, 3d Synod of Orleans, 538	• Law for the Protection of German Blood and Honor, September 15, 1935 (RGB1 I, 1146)
• Jews not permitted to show themselves in the streets during Passion Week, 3d Synod of Orleans, 538	• Decree authorizing local authorities to bar Jews from the streets on certain days (i.e. Nazi holidays), December 3, 1938 (RGB1 I, 1676)

CANONICAL LAW	NAZI MEASURE
• Burning of the Talmud and other books, 12th Synod of Toledo, 681	• Book burnings in Nazi Germany
• Christians not permitted to patronize Jewish doctors, Trulanic Synod, 692	• Decree of July 25, 1938 (RGB1 I, 969)
• Christians not permitted to live in Jewish homes, Synod of Narbonne, 1050	• Directive by Goring providing for concentration of Jews in houses, December 28, 1938 (Bormann to Rosenberg, January 17, 1939, PS–69)
• Jews obliged to pay taxes for support of church to the same extent as Christians, Synod of Gerona, 1078	• The "Sozialausgleichsabgabe" which provided that Jews pay a special income tax in lieu of donations for party purposes imposed on Nazis, December 24, 1940 (RGB1 I, 1666)
• Jews not permitted to be plaintiffs, or witnesses against Christians in courts, 3d Lateran Council, 1179, canon 26	• Proposal by the party chancellery that Jews not be permitted to institute civil suits, September 9, 1942 (Bormann to Justice Ministry, September 9, 1942, NG–151)
• Jews not permitted to withhold inheritance from descendants who accepted Christianity, 3d Lateran Council, 1179, canon 26	• Decree empowering the Justice Ministry to void wills offending the "sound judgment of the people," July 31, 1938 (RGB1 I, 937)
• The marking of Jewish clothes with a badge, 4th Lateran Council, 1215, canon 68 (Copied from the legislation by Caliph Omar II (634–44), who	• Decree of September 1, 1941 (RGB1 I, 547)

63

CANONICAL LAW	NAZI MEASURE
had decreed that Christians wear blue belts and Jews, yellow belts)	
• Construction of new synagogues prohibited, Council of Oxford, 1222	• Destruction of synagogues in entire Reich, November 10, 1938 (Heydrich to Goring, November 11, 1938, PS–3058)
• Christians not permitted to attend Jewish ceremonies, Synod of Vienna, 1267	• Friendly relations with Jews prohibited, October 24, 1941 (Gestapo directive, L–15)
• Compulsory ghettoes, Synod of Breslau, 1267	• Order by Heydrich, September 21, 1939 (PS–3363)
• Christians not permitted to sell or rent real estate to Jews, Synod of Ofen, 1279	• Decree providing for compulsory sale of Jewish real estate, December 3, 1938 (RGB1 I, 1709)
• Adoption by a Christian of the Jewish religion or return by a baptized Jew to the Jewish religion defined as heresy, Synod of Mainz, 1310	• Adoption by a Christian of the Jewish religion places him in jeopardy of being treated as a Jew. Decision by Oberlandesgericht Konigsberg, 4th Zivilsenant, June 26, 1942 (Die Judenfrage (Vertrauliche Beilage)
• Jews not permitted to act as agents in the conclusion of contracts between Christians, especially marriage contracts, Council of Basel, 1434, Sessio XIX	• Decree of July 6, 1938, providing for liquidation of Jewish real estate agencies, brokerage agencies, and marriage agencies catering to non-Jews (RGB1 I, 823)
• Jews not permitted to obtain academic degrees, Council of Basel, 1434, Sessio XIX	• Law against Overcrowding of German Schools and Universities, April 25, 1933 (RGB1 I, 225)[18]

The Jewish people have wandered throughout the world since they were driven from their land by the Romans in the first century. They have endured persecution and much heartache. The plight of the Jews over the centuries—especially during the Middle Ages, is captured in these poems by the German Jew, Moses Mendelssohn:

Wretched Jew; forced thus to wander,
Peddling wares through village and dale,
Poorly fed and shivering cold
Forever hawking: "Goods for sale."[19]

Collector: Three thalers, Jew, is what you must dole out.
Jew: Three thalers gold? Please, what's this all about?
Collector: You are a Jew! And that's the only reason:
     If you were an atheist, or even heathen
     We wouldn't take from you a single sou;
     But you pay through the nose, since you're a Jew!
Jew: Here, take your gold! Are these your Savior's teachings?[20]

This poem by W.H. Auden portrays the pain of German Jews who were forced to flee their German homeland during the Nazi reign of terror and endure rejection from nation after nation as they tried to find safety:

The consul banged the table and said,
  "If you've got no passport you're officially dead":
     But we are still alive, my dear, but we are still alive.

Saw a poodle in a jacket fastened with a pin,
 Saw a door opened and a cat let in:
But they weren't German Jews, my dear, but they weren't German Jews.[21]

In this poem, the German poet Heine captures the Jewish longing for a homeland within Germany, knowing that one day Germany would evict them as well—which it later did:

> I think of Germany at night
> The thought keeps me awake till light.

> I had, long since,
> a lovely fatherland.
> The oaks would gleam
> And touch the skies;
> the violet would nod.
> It was a dream.[22]

Wonderfully, in God's providence, the Jews are now coming
home to wander no more. After 1,900 years of wandering they have
their own homeland—this time it is not a dream. The Jewish people are in the midst of resurrection and no longer can we refer to
them as the "wandering Jews." Supernaturally, they have returned
to the place of their inheritance as they await a future awakening
through Messiah. God is once again breathing His holy breath into
their lungs, and Ezekiel's vision of the awakening of the valley of dry
bones is coming to pass. Could it be that in God's sovereign timing
our wandering has come to an end as well? We believe so. It is now
time after 1,900 long years of wandering away from the nourishing
Hebraic roots of our faith to come into our inheritance! A wonderful restorative resurrection awaits us. Keep reading to find out how.

FOUR

The Canary in the Coal Mine

We Go

Do not ask: Where?
We go.
We have been told to go
From the days of our fathers' fathers.
Abram went, Jacob went,
They all had to go,
Go to a land, go from a land,
All of them bent
Over the path of the farer,
Of those who never spared themselves,
All of them went, staff in the road-hard hand,
Promise in their hearts, eyes filled with Him,
Our God who bade us go on and on,
Turned to the one and only goal.
A hounded rest when he called a halt,
Strange farings from Nile to Rhine,

Long farings in dread
Until wells brim,
Meagre wells
For wavering, restless rest—
My roots reached down before those rooted
Who hunt me now, but I was a guest
In the land of others—always a guest.
Unthinkably long I rested there,
But never a rest that gives repose.
Our rest was drowned in tears and sweat and blood,
A sudden lightning and it cracked
In a cry:
Gone by, gone by!
In the full flare of sun—
We go.
Again He drives us,
Again He dooms us
To His eternal law:
To go on,
To go on!
The German Jewish Poet
Karl Wolfskehl, 1933

Deep within the hills of West Virginia tragedy often struck without warning. Early coal miners did not have the technology to help them detect toxic life threatening gases in new coal seams. Many miners lost their lives because the mines did not have ventilation systems. To save human lives they learned that if they would bring a caged canary into the mine with them, they could provide the sign of imminent catastrophe they sought. Canaries are ultra sensitive to methane and carbon monoxide gases. As long as the canary was singing the miners were safe. But should the canary stop singing and become faint or even die, the miners would have a small window of opportunity to escape with their lives. The canary became the centerpiece of life in the mine. You can imagine that every miner listened to the song of the canary. A silent canary cage was the sign of impending doom and a signal for immediate evacuation.

Early Warning Signs

Anti-Semitism within the church is like the canary in the coal mine. It acts as an early warning signal that something is tragically wrong. It is the sign that a gradual suffocation has begun that will eventually lead to a choking out of life. Certainly, God's promise to Abraham: "I will bless those who bless you and I will curse him who curses you" (Gen. 12:3) has come to pass over the centuries of time. Nations fall and rise based on their treatment of the chosen. The same is true for the church. The German evangelical church was the strongest in the world prior to World War II. Sadly, not heeding the early warning sign of anti-Semitism, the life of German Christianity was choked out. Today, a small percentage of German society makes claim to a born-again experience. The German church failed to notice the silence of the canary in the coal mine.

You might speculate that anti-Semitism is a small obscure issue within present day Christianity. But just as the death of one small, miniscule canary is a warning sign of a much larger problem, the same can be said of Christians who loathe Jews. Anti-Semitism has generally begun within the church and then spread to the society at large. As goes the church so goes the nation. Beginning with the tenets of Replacement Theology, anti-Semitism often takes root in the seminaries first then moves like a small brush fire to church pulpits. After church leaders begin fanning the flames of anti-Semitism, it becomes an acceptable worldview of that society. The questions before us in this chapter and the next are these: Is the church in America in danger? Is there a toxic life threatening anti-Semitism lurking in the church that we have not detected? If the church throughout the ages has succumbed to hatred and persecution of the Jews, will American Christians follow suit? Is the canary still singing?

As we have seen in Matthew 25, Jesus promised that at the end of the age He would separate the gentile nations as a shepherd separates the sheep from the goats based on their treatment of His brethren—the Jewish people: We are living at the end of the age. A revolution of separation is happening the world over. No, the Jews are not being forced by the church to wear a yellow Star of David on their clothing—yet, but a general loathing of Jews in many Christian circles around the world has begun. A line is being drawn in the sand, and the church is once again falling into the flames of Jewish hatred and separating themselves from the chosen people of God. Out of these venomous flames the false church will arise and pave the way for the Antichrist. In speaking of the last days Jesus said: "Then they will deliver you up to tribulation and kill you, and you will be hated by all nations for My name's sake" (Matt. 24:9). The gentile nations will follow the leanings of the false church and meet their doom at the end of the age when the Son of Man separates them from Himself for eternity because of their mistreatment of His brethren, the Jews.

Moving silently at first—like the methane toxic gas in a coal mine—this revolution of separation will ultimately grow into a powerfully influential movement that will deceive many. Using political correctness as its main weapon of choice, the revolution of separation will have widespread acceptance in both geopolitical and religious circles. Even now within the halls of church leadership circles worldwide, an anti-Jewish mentality is becoming commonplace. Several mainline American denominations have divested their investments from any business that sells products to Israel. In a later chapter we will see that Scripture is very clear that during the final moments of history all nations will turn against the chosen people of God. The fullness of Satan's fury will of course be unleashed against the Jews through the Antichrist but leading up to this future holocaust will be a gradual breakdown of commitment to the Jewish people. Nations that once stood by Israel will reject her. Deep within the halls of church denominations and theological institutions there will grow a deep divide and distaste of the Jews. Make no mistake—a revolution of separation is approaching that will seal the eternal fate of multitudes. As churches and nations separate themselves from God's covenant people they will do so in opposition to God Himself. Jesus is saying in Matthew 25 that to reject the Jews is to reject Him: "Inasmuch as you did not do it to one of the least of these [My brethren—the Jewish people], you did not do it to Me" (Matt. 25:45). To separate oneself from the Jews is to reject Jesus Himself! This great separation will seal the fate of the unrighteous.

A Rising Remnant of Righteous Gentiles from the Nations

However, Jesus also speaks about a group of righteous Gentiles in Matthew 25 who minister to His chosen people at the end of the age. His response to these righteous Gentiles of the nations is very loving: "Then the King will say to those on His right hand, 'Come, you blessed of My Father, inherit the kingdom prepared for you from the foundation of the world'" (Matt. 25:34). Could it be that these righteous Gentiles are blessed by the Father because of a fulfillment of God's promise to Abraham in Genesis 12:3: "I will bless those who bless you?" We wholeheartedly believe so.

A wonderful blessing awaits all who will pay attention to the warning signs of Jewish hatred—no matter how small and insignificant. As we will see, the signs are all around us. Like her European predecessors the church in America is stirring the flames of anti-Semitism. The canary is silent but it's not too late to flee to safety. The revolution of separation has begun in America. The two minute warning alarm has sounded. Only righteous Gentiles will be able to withstand the pressures of this hour. A wonderful end-time promise of the Father's blessing awaits every believer who will minister to and protect the Jews. As Jesus separates those who love His brethren

71

from those who hate them, will you be in the company of the righteous who stand with the Jews in the final hour? Will you be loyal to Jesus and obey His Word in the power of the Holy Spirit—even if it is not popular or politically correct to do so?

History Keeps Repeating Itself

The facts you are about to read in this chapter and the next may shock you. They will prove that many American Christian leaders are avoiding the lessons of history and fanning the flames of anti-Semitism. We lovingly plead with these Christian leaders to reconsider their views concerning Israel and the Jewish people.

George Santayana said: "Those who cannot learn from history are doomed to repeat it." George Bernard Shaw said: "We learn from history that we learn nothing from history." Not to dull you with history quotes, we give you one more from Rudyard Kipling: "As it will be in the future, it was at the birth of man. There are only four things certain since social progress began. That the dog returns to his vomit and the sow returns to her mire. And the burnt fool's bandaged finger goes wobbling back to the fire."

Are the same mistakes that led the church in the Middle Ages to produce inquisitions, pogroms (the violent destruction of Jewish communities) and yellow patches, repeating themselves in the American church today? Are the embers still smoldering that led baptized Christians to massacre six million innocents in Europe during the Holocaust? Are the grey ashes from the gas chambers catching fire in the nation we hold dear? Is the "burnt fool's bandaged finger wobbling back to the fire?"

Tragically it is true. A grassroots anti-Semitic movement has begun among American evangelicals and mainline Protestants. Just like the dead canary in the coal mine—anti-Semitism is a warning sign of a deadly problem lurking in the wings. Listen to these heartfelt words from *The Crucifixion of the Jews*, by Franklin H. Littell:

A rise of anti-Semitism is often the first seismographic reading on a serious shift and shearing along the fault lines of bedrock Christianity. The fundamental fault line of false teaching about the Jewish people, anti-Semitism serves a useful purpose to individuals insecure in their personal identity and to groups uncertain of their present and future prospects. It is therefore indicative of a broader and deeper malaise in the society.... The rise of modern political anti-Semitism in the last century is thus a measure of the churches' failure to minister as well as to teach truthfully about the Jews. Not only the blood of the Jews but the blood of ill-trained and ill-served apostates must therefore be charged to the current account of Christendom.....The anti-Semite is a criminal in his heart and a coward in his public conduct.... Toward the helpless which in Christendom has usually meant the Jews, he directs a veritable torrent of contempt, hatred and—when permitted—violence....The Jew gives the anti-Semite his identity as a kind of antimatter; his anxiety and self-hate is polarized in tension toward the one marked as a carrier of history. The Jew, even if confused as an individual has a historical identity. Even if he denies his faith, a Jew nevertheless has a rendezvous with his Jewish destiny. Even if you flee from that destiny, it pursues you. The anti-Semite acquires a fleeting identity parasitically.[1]

Londonistan

Before we investigate the evidence of anti-Semitism within the American church, let's take a quick look at the church in Great Britain. You might say that what is happening in England—in London in particular—is indicative of what is about to happen in America if we don't learn from England's errors. For us, England could be seen as a canary in a coal mine—a warning signal that the same fate awaits the American church if we don't challenge those who inspire Jewish hatred among us. An eye opening book that chronicles the downward spiral into the abyss of Jew loathing within British Christianity is entitled *Londonistan*. Its author is Melanie Phillips. Melanie is a graduate in English from Oxford University and is a contributor of a regular column to the daily Mail. She has also published in the *Guardian, Observer, Sunday Times,* and *Spectator.* Melanie also received the Orwell Prize for Journalism in 1996. The strange title *Londonistan* is explained by Melanie in the introduction to the book:

> The London bombings (in July 2005) revealed a terrible truth about Britain, something even more alarming and dangerous to America's long-term future than the fact that foreign terrorists had been able to carry out the 9/11 attacks on U.S. soil in 2001. They finally lifted the veil on Britain's dirty secret in the war on terrorism—that for more than a decade, London had been the epicenter of Islamic militancy in Europe. Under the noses of successive British governments, Britain's capital had turned into "Londonistan"—a mocking play on the names of such state sponsors of terrorism as Afghanistan—and become the major European center for the promotion, recruitment and financing of Islamic terror and extremism. Indeed, it could be argued that it was in London that al-Qaeda was first forged from disparate radical groups into a global terrorist phenomenon. During the 1980s and 1990s, despite repeated protests from other countries around the world, Londonistan flourished virtually without public comment at home—and, most remarkably of all, with no attempt at all to combat it by the governmental and intelligence agencies that were all too aware of what was happening. Incredibly, London had become the hub of the European terror networks.[2]

Phillips shows that at the center of England's downfall is a church that sympathizes with radical Islam: "Far from defending the nation at the heart of whose identity and values its own doctrines lie, the Church of England—Britain's established church—has internalized the hatred of the West that defines the shared universe of radical Islamism and the revolutionary left. At a clergy gathering on 9/11, as clerics watched the horror unfold on a large TV screen, one turned to another and said: 'I hope Bush doesn't retaliate. The West has brought this judgment on itself.'"[3]

What would inspire a church leader to say such a thing? Phillips believes that it is because of a drastic change in the worldview of believing Christians:

The outcome for the Church has been that faith in God and belief in the fundamental doctrines of Christianity have been replaced by worship of social liberalism. The Church stopped trying to save people's souls and started trying instead to change society. It signed up to the prevailing doctrine of the progressive class that the world's troubles were caused by poverty, oppression and discrimination. Miracles were replaced by Marx. Accordingly, it soaked up the radical message coming out of the World Council of Churches, under the influence of liberation theology, that the problems of the poor peoples of the south were social and economic, and emanated from the capitalist West and America in particular.[4]

A church that mixes sympathy for Islam and radical Marxist Liberation Theology is in grave danger. Soon it will give way to anti-Semitism because it is the natural result of that deadly marriage of ideologies. Phillips shows that this is what happened in Britain:

The result is a virulent animosity towards Israel in the established Churches in Britain, which promulgate inflammatory libels against it.... the ACC (Anglican Consultative Council) also endorsed an accompanying report by the Anglican Peace and Justice Network, a piece of venomous and mendacious Palestinian propaganda that provided a travesty of both history and present reality. Ignoring the offer by Israel in 2000 of a state of Palestine based on more than 90 percent of the disputed territories, it asserted that "there have been no significant positive steps towards the creation of the state of Palestine. On the contrary, the state of Israel has systematically and deliberately oppressed and dehumanized the people of Palestine." It presented Israel's military actions as a deliberate policy of oppression which had made Palestinian lives a misery, whereas the only reason that normal Palestinian life was impossible was the Palestinian war of terror against Israel. It described Israel's security barrier as an "apartheid/segregation" wall and compared the territories to the "Bantustans of South Africa," despite the fact that the Arabs in Israel have full civil rights and the Arabs outside Israel are by definition not its citizens. Most egregiously of all, it compared "the concrete walls of Palestine" to the "barbed-wire fence of the Buchenwald camp." Thus the Anglicans compared the Jews of Israel to the Nazis on account of a measure that aimed to prevent them from being murdered. In February 2006, there was a repeat performance. This time, the Synod backed a call from the Episcopal Church in Jerusalem and the Middle East for the Church Commissioners to divest from "Companies profiting from the illegal occupation," such as Caterpillar Inc. An American company, Caterpillar manufactures bulldozers used by Israel in clearance projects in the disputed territories.[5]

What does Melanie Phillips believe contributes to this anti-Israel bias within the Church of England? What does she believe is the warning sign that went unheeded by the church? What was the canary in the coal mine that created the deafening silence that no one in the church heard?

The real motor behind the Church's engine of Israeli delegitimization is theology—or, to be more precise, the resurgence of a particular theology that had long been officially consigned to ignominy. This is "replacement theology," sometimes known also as "supercessionism," a doctrine going back to the early Church Fathers and stating that all God's promises to the Jews—including the land of Israel—were forfeit because the Jews had denied the divinity of Christ. This doctrine lay behind centuries of Christian anti-Jewish hatred until the Holocaust drove it underground.... Moreover, replacement theology is not just a form of anti-Zionism; it directly attacks Jewish religion, history and identity....According to Canon Andrew White, replacement theology is dominant in the Church of England and present in almost every church, fueling the venom against Israel. Lord Carey agrees that replacement theology is the most important driver behind the Church's hatred of Israel.[6]

The True and False Church

Bernard Shaw was right in saying "We learn from history that we learn nothing from history." The rhetoric coming out of the

Church of England is no different than the virulent anti-Jewish language of the past 1,900 years. The burnt fool's bandaged finger is wobbling back to the fire. From what we have learned from history in this section on the revolution of separation, it should come as no surprise that a future anti-Semitism will once again be embraced by the gentile church. This time around however, it will be more vile and thirsty for Jewish blood than any other time in history. This will be due to the full unveiling of the end-time spirit of Antichrist. Two kinds of churches are emerging in the world: The true church (the righteous Gentiles that Jesus commends in Matthew 25) that will embrace the Jews and the false church that will reject the Jews. One church will be apostolic and the other apostate.

Time is short. If you desire to have understanding of the times in which we live, ask the Holy Spirit to reveal these things to you. Search the Scriptures to see if what we are saying is true. Don't accept the belief that God has rejected the Jews forever because a leading scholar says so or because of a fondness for the writings of a particular church father. Ask the Holy Spirit to guide you into the truth. These are critical days for the church in America. We cannot miss it on this issue. If we do, we will follow in the footsteps of the Church of England and the church of Germany and eventually suffocate. How we stand on this one issue of our love or rejection of Jewish people the world over is the greatest issue facing the church today. As we will see in coming chapters, our restoration to the Jewish people as a whole and particularly to the Messianic Jewish remnant, is the key to the end-time world harvest of souls. Right now though, let's look to see if anti-Semitism is gaining acceptance in American Christianity.

A Face in the Window

Men never do evil so completely and cheerfully
as when they do it from a religious conviction.
Blaise Pascal

In His Novel: *The Town Beyond the Wall*, Elie Wiesel tells the story of the deportation of Jews from a small town in Hungary during the Holocaust. A teenage boy and his family are herded with the rest of the Jews into the main courtyard of the synagogue to await transport to the death camps. Across the way the young man sees a face in the window—a spectator—watching the horror without expression:

I can still see him, that Saturday. Jews were filling the courtyard. On their backs they carried whatever they had saved of a lifetime of work. Knapsacks into which the old had stuffed their past, the children their future, the rabbis their faith, the sick their exhaustion. The wandering Jew was about to set out again, the exile's staff in his hand. The wandering Jew was headed toward the "final solution." At last the world was to be

relieved of the great problem that had haunted it for two thousand years!
Now at last it would be able to breathe!

No one in the crowd was crying. No one wailed or even spoke.
Ghosts, thronging up from the depths of history. Fearful, silent ghosts.
They awaited the order to move out. Hungarian police, black feathers in
their hats, came and went, rifles at the ready, bludgeons poised.

My parents and I stood close to the fence: on the other side were
life and liberty, or what men call life and liberty. A few passers-by; they
averted their faces; the more sensitive bowed their heads.

It was then that I saw him. A face in the window across the way. The
curtains hid the rest of him; only his head was visible. It was like a balloon.
Bald, flat nose, wide empty eyes. A bland face, banal, bored: no passion
ruffled it. I watched it for a long time. It was gazing out, reflecting no pity,
no pleasure, no shock, not even anger or interest. Impassive, cold, imper-
sonal. The face was indifferent to the spectacle. What? Men are going to
die? That's not my fault, is it now? I didn't make the decision. The face is
neither Jewish nor anti-Jewish; a simple spectator, that's what it is.

For seven days the great courtyard of the synagogue filled and emp-
tied. He, standing behind the curtains, watched. The police beat women
and children; he did not stir. It was no concern of his. He was neither
victim nor executioner; a spectator, that's what he was. He wanted to live
in peace and quiet.

His face, empty of all expression, followed me for long years. I have
forgotten many others; not his…I felt neither hate nor anger toward him:
simply curiosity. I did not understand him. How can anyone remain a
spectator indefinitely? How can anyone continue to embrace the women
he loves, to pray to God with fervor if not faith, to dream of a better
tomorrow—after having seen that? After having glimpsed the precise line
dividing life from death and good from evil?

80

The others, all the others, were he. The third in the triangle. Between victims and executioners there is a mysterious bond; they belong to the same universe; one is the negation of the other. The Germans' logic was clear, comprehensible to the victims. Even evil and madness show a stunted intelligence.

But this is not true of the other. The spectator is entirely beyond us. He sees without being seen. He is there but unnoticed. The footlights hide him. He neither applauds nor hisses; his presence is evasive, and commits him less than his absence might. He says neither yes nor no, and not even maybe. He says nothing. He is there, but he acts as if he were not. Worse: he acts as if the rest of us were not.[1]

How will Christians respond to the coming wave of anti-Semitism in America? As many theologians, denominational heads, and pastors, buy into the old beliefs of Replacement Theology, will Christians remain silent? Will we become another expressionless face in the window—impassive and impersonal spectators of the coming holocaust toward Jews? Or, will we search the Scriptures to discover if what these men and women are saying is really true? Will we allow the Holy Spirit to guide us into truth? Will we put the proverbial foot down and say, "Never again will we accept anti-Semitism within the church! We will be loyal to the Lord and His brethren—our elder Jewish brothers and sisters?" Will we join the ranks of many godly Gentiles throughout the ages who have defended and sheltered Jewish people the world over? We pray to that end. The end-time church will fall into two categories: apostate or apostolic—there will be no room for compromise on the issue of the church and the Jews.

A Most Surprising Turn of Events

The very thought of indifference toward Jewish people is most likely troubling to you. Christian anti-Semitism in America? Unheard of? Unthinkable? Yes, it is quite true. Who are the ones promoting Christian anti-Judaism in the land we love? The answer will surprise you. These are not men and women who must cloak their views in fear of public backlash. On the contrary, they are dredging up the old anti-Jewish doctrines of Justin Martyr and John Chrysostom and trying to make them palatable once again. Following the playbook of the Church of England they are bringing anti-Semitism into the mainstream of Christian thought and have captured the attention of a wide audience. In fact, the tenets of Replacement/Supercessionist Theology have been embraced and endorsed by American Christians from all traditions—mainstream, evangelicals and charismatics. Yes—we are unwittingly repeating history in our time because we have failed to learn from it.

Most shockingly, the leaders of this anti-Jewish movement are dynamic men and women of God—sterling leaders of character and depth. Several of them we know personally and call them friends. They include evangelical graduate school and seminary professors, members of the National Association of Evangelicals, denominational heads, presidents of para-church organizations, seminary presidents and pastors of large influential congregations. This organized anti-Israel movement within the American church is moving quickly beyond an underground grass roots effort. It is now (as in the Middle Ages and the days of the Holocaust) part of the worldview of many churches in America. Funny how the shameful sins of our collective past come crashing back into our time and we fail to recognize the connection. Because of a growing anti-Semitism, the church in Germany accepted Nazi fundamentalism and allowed—even facilitated—the murder of six million Jews. Because of anti-Semitism the Church of England accepted Islamic fundamentalism, promoted the Palestinian cause over Israel and inspired a country to believe in the Muslim terrorist propaganda that the Jews are responsible for the world's ills. Today, the country of England is cowering under the pressure of constant threat of terror from within her own borders. Over two million Muslim fundamentalists have been allowed to immigrate to her shores.

Connecting the Dots

Today, it is not a Nazi fascist dictator telling us that the Jews are the cause of the problems in the world. Rather, it's one of many Islamic fascist dictators telling us the Jews are responsible for the problems in the world. It is the same message, just a different messenger. It is the same lie, just a different liar. The repetition of this cycle is uncanny. Something cataclysmic happens in a nation: a drought, the black plague, an economic downturn, a war, a terrorist attack, a regional conflict, and someone has to be blamed. We can't blame God because He's unseen, so we attack His chosen representatives—the Jews. In order to pin the blame on someone and make sense of the chaos, church leaders dredge from the abyss the old ideas of Justin Martyr and make scapegoats of the Jews. They re-package Replacement/Supercessionist Theology to fit their particular crisis, dust it off and proclaim it to the masses. The church accepts the propaganda and soon the lie goes public and the secular nation buys into it. Out come the yellow stars of David, the pogroms begin, and the Jews are kicked out of the country—or worse yet: segregated into ghettos, shot, burned, starved, put into the racks, blown up in buses, or gassed—depending on what time period the pogrom occurs: ancient, medieval, modern or postmodern. Sometimes the Jews are left in the miserable position of waiting for a future punishment of some kind while enduring constant acts of violence that the church ignores.

Like Esther and Mordecai of old, the Jews throughout the centuries have had to ward off the evil judgments decreed by Haman-like church leaders. By the end of the Inquisition, pogrom, or Holocaust, the church that is responsible for acts of terror against the Jewish people sinks into a dreadful night and the sponsoring nation crumbles.

What's so unnerving about this unending cycle is that so far, no one seems to pick up on the tragedy of it all. Kipling was right: "The dog returns to his vomit and the sow returns to her mire, and the burnt fool's bandaged finger goes wobbling back to the fire." And sadly, few bother to connect the historical dots that prove the greatest sponsor of worldwide terror against the Jewish race has been the church. The painful fact that we all must face is that the people who have suffered most over the centuries for their faith in the God of Abraham, Isaac, and Jacob have been Jews.

It would be impossible to record all of the signs that the toxic fumes of anti-Semitism have penetrated the American church. Following are a few of the more pronounced examples:

Letter to the President from Evangelical Leaders

In the summer of 2007, a group of thirty-four evangelical leaders sent a letter to then president of the United States, George Bush. Soon after, the letter along with the names of its authors was published in the New York Times. Here is the letter in its entirety:

Dear Mr. President:

We write as evangelical Christian leaders in the United States to thank you for your efforts (including the major address on July 16) to reinvigorate the Israeli-Palestinian negotiations to achieve a lasting peace in the region. We affirm your clear call for a two-state solution. We urge that your administration not grow weary in the time it has left in office to utilize the vast influence of America to demonstrate creative, consistent and determined U.S. leadership to create a new future for Israelis and Palestinians. We pray to that end, Mr. President.

We also write to correct a serious misperception among some people including some U.S. policymakers that all American evangelicals are opposed to a two-state solution and creation of a new Palestinian state that includes the vast majority of the West Bank. Nothing could be further from the truth. We, who sign this letter, represent large numbers of evangelicals throughout the U.S. who support justice for both Israelis and Palestinians. We hope this support will embolden you and your administration to proceed confidently and forthrightly in negotiations with both sides in the region.

As evangelical Christians, we embrace the biblical promise to Abraham: "I will bless those who bless you" (Genesis 12:3). And precisely as evangelical Christians committed to the full teaching of the Scriptures, we know that blessing and loving people (including Jews and the present State of Israel) does not mean withholding criticism when it is warranted. Genuine love and genuine blessing means acting in ways that promote the genuine and long-term well being of our neighbors. Perhaps the best way we can bless Israel is to encourage her to remember, as she deals with her neighbor Palestinians, the profound teaching on justice that the Hebrew prophets proclaimed so forcefully as an inestimably precious gift to the whole world.

Historical honesty compels us to recognize that both Israelis and Palestinians have legitimate rights stretching back for millennia to the lands of Israel/Palestine. Both Israelis and Palestinians have committed violence and injustice against each other. The only way to bring the tragic cycle of violence to an end is for Israelis and Palestinians to negotiate a just, lasting agreement that guarantees both sides viable independent, secure states. To achieve that goal, both sides must give up some of the competing, incompatible claims. Israelis and Palestinians must both accept each other's right to exist and to achieve that goal, the U.S. must provide robust leadership within the Quartet to reconstitute the Middle East roadmap, whose full implementation would guarantee the security of the State of Israel and the viability of a Palestinian State. We affirm the new role of former Prime Minister Tony Blair and pray that the conference you plan for this fall will be a success.

Mr. President, we renew our prayers and support for your leadership to help bring peace to Jerusalem, and justice and peace for all the people in the Holy land.

Finally, we would request to meet with you to personally convey our support and discuss other ways in which we may help your administration on this crucial issue.[2]

At first glance, one would think these evangelical leaders are simply voicing the concern that Israelis and Palestinians end the violence of the Middle East conflict. We commend these leaders for their stated purpose of being "committed to the full teaching of the Scriptures." We are also happy that they "embrace the biblical promise to Abraham." How then is it possible for them to call for the "full implementation" of the roadmap to peace which has as its main purpose the dividing of the land of Israel? God's promise to Abraham in Genesis 17:8 declares that the land in its entirety belongs to the Jewish people forever: "Also I give to you and your descendants after you the land in which you are a stranger; all the land of Canaan, as an everlasting possession; and I will be their God."

As well, how can one argue with the promise God gives to Israel through the prophet Jeremiah? In this promise, God makes it very clear that the very ordinances of the earth and heavens—the sun, moon, stars, and roaring seas are proof that His covenant with Israel as a nation has not been broken: "Thus says the Lord, who gives the sun for a light by day, the ordinances of the moon and the stars for a light by night, who disturbs the sea, and its waves roar (the Lord of hosts is His name): 'If those ordinances depart from before Me, says the Lord, then the seed of Israel shall also cease from being a nation before Me forever'" (Jer. 31:35–36).

The roadmap to peace supported by a quartet of nations calls for Israel to give up more of their God ordained land for peace. This divestment of land requires Israel to give away the Gaza (which they have already done—reaping more acts of terror); the West Bank—including Hebron—the land Abraham purchased to bury Sarah; the Golan Heights; and half of Jerusalem—the City of David. For these Christian leaders to call for the dividing of God's land is to annul the covenant God made with Abraham rather than embrace it. God swore two irrevocable and unconditional oaths to Abraham:

1. To "bless" or redeem the world through his seed (Gen. 12:1–3), and
2. To give the promised land of Canaan to Abraham and his natural descendants as an "everlasting possession" (Gen. 17:8).

An Everlasting Covenant

God chose the Jewish people and the land of Israel for the purpose of world redemption. Today, the Jewish people and the land are at the epicenter of world events as they unfold in the last days. We sincerely ask the thirty-four evangelical leaders who signed this letter to the president: by whose authority do you nullify and erase the promise God gave to Abraham? King David, writing one thousand years after this land promise was given to Abraham recalls it and affirms it in the Psalms: "He remembers His covenant forever, the word which He commanded, for a thousand generations. The covenant which He made with Abraham, and His oath to Isaac, and confirmed it to Jacob for a statue, to Israel as an everlasting covenant, saying, 'To you I will give the land of Canaan as the allotment of your inheritance'" (Ps. 105:8–11).

Nowhere in the Scripture is there an oath or promise that God breaks. He is always faithful to His covenantal promises. Some would say that God breaks His covenants based on our lack of faith. Paul the Apostle would say no: "If we are faithless, He remains faithful; He cannot deny Himself" (2 Tim. 2:13). In speaking of the Jews, Paul declares in Romans 3:3–4: "For what if some did not believe? Will their unbelief make the faithfulness of God without effect? Certainly not! Indeed, let God be true but every man a liar."

In other words, if some Jews do not believe in Jesus it does not nullify God's eternal promise to them. Again, in Galatians, Paul, the Jewish apostle, affirms all of the promises God gave to Abraham—which includes the land of Israel for eternity. He makes it very clear that no one can nullify the land promise because it was given before the law and confirmed with an oath by God:

Brethren, I speak in the manner of men: Though it is only a man's covenant, yet if it is confirmed, no one annuls or adds to it. Now to Abraham and his Seed were the promises made. He does not say, "And to seeds," as of many, but as of one, "And to your Seed," who is Christ. And this I say that the law, which was four hundred and thirty years later, cannot annul the covenant that was confirmed before by God in Christ, *that it should make the promise of no effect. For if the inheritance is of the law, it is no longer of promise; but God gave it to Abraham by promise* (Gal. 3:15–18).

Yes, it is true that in the Mosaic covenant, God placed conditions on Israel's right to live in the land. God foreknew that Israel would break His commandments and be scattered across the face of the earth. Yet, even in judgment He promised to remember the land covenant He made with them. In judgment God remembers mercy:

Then I will remember My covenant with Jacob, and My covenant with Isaac, and My covenant with Abraham I will remember; I will remember the land. The land also shall be left empty by them, and will enjoy its Sabbaths while it lies desolate without them; they will accept their guilt, because their soul abhorred My statutes. Yet for all that, when they are in the land of their enemies, I will not cast them away, nor shall I abhor them to utterly destroy them and break My covenant with them; for I am the Lord their God (Lev. 26:42–45).

God Never Breaks a Promise!

For these evangelical leaders to question God's covenants and declare them annulled seems to undermine our salvation. Hear the words of the Scriptures:

For when God made a promise to Abraham, because He could swear by no one greater, He swore by Himself, saying, "Surely blessing I will bless you, and multiplying I will multiply you." And so, after he had patiently endured, he obtained the promise. For men indeed swear by the greater, and an oath for confirmation is for them an end of all dispute. Thus God, determining to show more abundantly to the heirs of promise the immutability of His counsel, confirmed it by an oath, that by two immutable things, in which it is impossible for God to lie, we might have strong consolation, who have fled for refuge to lay hold of the hope set before us. This hope we have as an anchor of the soul, both sure and steadfast (Heb. 6:13–19).

If God is unfaithful to His covenants to Israel how can we trust Him to be faithful to His promises to us? How can we who have fled for refuge to the Son of God have any hope that our salvation is an anchor of our souls? If God has annulled His covenants to Abraham then the New Covenant in Jesus can be annulled as well. But God has not broken any of His promises—ever. Nor will He.

These leaders state that they are compelled by "historical honesty." But yet the Jewish people have been attached to this land for four thousand years. In this land the Jews became a nation and wrote the Scriptures. Most importantly, the Jewish Messiah, Jesus, was born on this hallowed ground. Now, after 1,900 years of prophesied Diaspora (dispersion), God—true to His Word—is bringing His people back to their own land.

Confronting the Choice of the God of Israel

As we have seen in Matthew 25, the response of the nations toward Israel is in direct alignment with their response toward the God of Israel. To reject the nation of Israel is to reject God Himself. This letter to the president is actually calling for the dividing of the promised land of Israel God gave to the Hebrew people. The words of Jesus in Matthew 25 affirm what God spoke through the prophets Joel and Zephaniah concerning those who would be so bold as to divide His covenantal land: "I will also gather all nations, and will bring them down into the valley of Jehoshaphat, and will plead with them there for My people and for my heritage Israel, whom they have scattered among the nations, and parted My land" (Joel 3:2). "Therefore wait ye upon Me, says the Lord, until the day that I rise up to the prey: for My determination is to gather the nations, that I may assemble the kingdoms, to pour upon them Mine indignation…" (Zeph. 3:8).

In our day, a great agitation is stirring in the nations of the earth. The Scriptures are clear that this age will not end until all of the nations will lay siege against Israel and the city of Jerusalem to divide her (see Zech. 12:1–9). The entire world will once and for all be confronted with God's sovereign choice of Israel:

Thus says the Lord, who stretches out the heavens, lays the foundation of the earth, and forms the spirit of man within him: "Behold, I will make Jerusalem a cup of drunkenness to all the surrounding peoples, when they lay siege against Judah and Jerusalem. And it shall happen in that day that I will make Jerusalem a very heavy stone for all peoples; all who would heave it away will surely be cut in pieces, though all nations of the earth are gathered against it" (Zech. 12:1–3).

For I will gather all the nations to battle against Jerusalem… the Lord will go forth and fight against those nations, as He fights in the day of battle, and in that day His feet will stand on the Mount of Olives, which faces Jerusalem on the east. And the Mount of Olives shall be split in two, from east to west, making a very large valley; half of the mountain shall move toward the north and half of it toward the south (Zech. 14:2–4).

This valley that Zechariah speaks of has not been formed yet. When Jesus, the Jewish Messiah returns to Jerusalem He will set His feet upon the Mount of Olives causing a great earthquake that will form a large valley. This is the place where Jesus will judge the nations of the earth based on whether or not they accepted His divine choice of Jacob's seed. Joel adds to the prophetic significance of this valley: "Multitudes, multitudes in the valley of decision! For the day of the Lord is near in the valley of decision…the Lord also will roar from Zion, and utter His voice from Jerusalem; The heavens and earth will shake but the Lord will be a shelter for His people, and the strength of the children of Israel" (Joel 3:14, 16).

A Battle over Ideology Not Real Estate

The spirit of this letter to the President is that the Jews are responsible for the Middle East conflict. The letter seems to say: If the

Jews would give up more land and treat the Palestinians with more love, dignity, and justice, then the bloodshed would stop. However, the Middle East conflict is not about land. It never has been. For the lovers of history here are a few key facts that are often overlooked:

Between 1914–1918 the world was plunged into the Great War. The Allies (mainly France, Britain, Russia; and the United States) fought against the Central Powers (Germany, Austria-Hungary, and the Turkish Ottoman Empire). After the war, the map of the world was changed dramatically. A significant shift of land sovereignty took place in the Middle East. Up until World War I the entire Middle East had been under the control of the Turkish Ottoman Empire for four hundred years. The Allied powers agreed to split the empire into two—giving half to France (the French Mandate) and the other half to England (the British Mandate). Keep in mind that prior to this time Syria, Lebanon, Iraq, Saudi Arabia—among other present nations of the Middle East—were not born yet.

The British Mandate encompassed the West Bank of the Jordan River to the Mediterranean Sea. It also included land on the East Bank of the Jordan called Trans-Jordan. Picking up on what the Romans called this land after they destroyed Jerusalem, the British named it "Palestine." The land was a no man's land. The Turks charged property taxes based on the number of trees one had on their land. Thus, the Ottoman subjects cut down the majority of vegetation in the empire leaving the land a desolate swamp filled with malaria. When Mark Twain visited this territory in the late 1800s, he recorded that he could count the trees with the fingers of his two hands. At this time there were approximately one hundred thousand Jews living in the land of Israel. Arabs who came to this desolate region were motivated by the employment offered by Jews in building and farming. By the time large numbers of Jews began arriving in the land in 1882, only a small number (two hundred and fifty thousand) Arabs lived there.

After the Great War, Jewish people the world over believed their hope in a homeland was now possible. A person who played a key role in opening the door to this dream was a Jew named Chaim Weizmann. Weizmann's invention of artificial acetone—the chief ingredient in gunpowder—contributed to Great Britain's victory in the war. The British offered Chaim a sizeable monetary payment for his efforts which he declined. Instead, he asked for the return of the homeland of his people.

The British government secretary assigned to oversee the land within the borders of the British Mandate was Arthur James Balfour. In God's providence, Balfour was told the stories of the Hebrew people by his God-fearing mother as a young boy. She proclaimed to him from an early age that one day the Jews would return to the land of Israel according to God's Word. Balfour's mother believed the covenant God gave to Abraham was eternal and unbreakable. Balfour has become a stunning example of a righteous Gentile who God dramatically raised up to sustain and protect His covenant people. History was made on November 2, 1917 when in a letter to Lord Rothchild Balfour declared: "His Majesty's government looks with favor upon the establishment in Palestine of a national homeland for the Jewish people." This became known as the "Balfour Declaration." In Balfour's decree, the British promised the Jewish people a homeland that encompassed all of Israel west of the Jordan to the Mediterranean, plus the area east of the Jordan known as Trans-Jordan. Think of it! A gentile Christian played a key role in Israel's restoration to her land. In the end however, Great Britain capitulated to Arab pressure and forgot their promise to the Jews. Tran-Jordan (today the country of Jordan) was given to Hussein Sherif of Mecca—thus removing seventy-five percent of the land of promise.

In 1964 Yasser Arafat formed a branch of terrorism known as the Palestinian Liberation Organization (PLO). The objective of the movement was to annihilate the Jews and find a home for the refugees from the war of 1948. Somehow, Arafat came to the conclusion that Israel was the ancient national homeland of the refugee population. He coined a new name for this new found people group: "Palestinians."

It is interesting that it was only after Israel was re-established as a nation that the myth of a Palestinian nation began to gain international attention. Palestinians did not come from "Judea"—Jews did. There has never been a Palestinian language or culture. Up until Yasser Arafat began proclaiming a historic link to this hallowed ground, there was never a nation of Palestine governed by Palestinians. Israel became a nation two thousand years before the birth of Islam in about 1300 BCE. The Jews have been in dominion over the land for a total of one thousand years and have had an unending presence there for three thousand three hundred years. As well, Jerusalem has been the Jewish capital for over three thousand three hundred years, but has never once been an Arab or Muslim capital. Furthermore, the city of Jerusalem is named 669 times in the Jewish Bible. The word Zion, which always stands for Jerusalem or the land of Israel, is mentioned 144 times. The New Testament Scriptures mention Jerusalem 154 times and Zion seven times. If the city of Jerusalem is truly a Palestinian capital and if the land of Israel should be broken up and given to others as the signers of this letter demand, then there should be some mention of Jerusalem in the Koran—the holy book of Islam. Not surprisingly, the Koran never mentions Jerusalem. In fact, in the Palestinian charter, written by Yasser Arafat, Jerusalem is not mentioned.

For the last forty years the PLO and other Arab terrorist groups have terrorized the people of Israel through countless suicide attacks, murder, and shelling of innocent men, women, and children. The world thinks the dispute is about land, but history proves otherwise. Interestingly, from 1949 to 1967 the West Bank, Jerusalem, and Gaza were under Arab control. In the Six Day War of 1967, Israel was again attacked by her Arab neighbors. Again, miraculously, Israel won the war and gained control of the West Bank, Jerusalem, and Gaza. Why didn't the Arabs form a homeland state for the refugees in the years that they occupied this land?

The tiny state of Israel is about the size of New Jersey. Twenty two Arab and Islamic nations surround Israel. Arab countries have a total land mass that is 640 times the size of Israel. By population, Arabs outnumber Jews fifty to one. If you were to look at a map of the Middle East that includes both Israel and the Arab/Islamic world, you would be hard pressed to locate tiny Israel. The conflict in the Middle East is not about land. It's about Islamic fundamentalism's mission to exterminate Jews whether they live on twenty thousand square miles or twenty acres. This is not a dispute about real estate. It's a dispute about Jews. The ultimate goal of Islam is to rid the entire world of Jews, and Israel is the first line of defense.

The two state solution these evangelical leaders say will provide a "lasting agreement that guarantees both sides a viable independence" with peace and security offers no guarantees whatsoever. A two state solution was rejected by the Palestinians at Camp David in 2000. For the PLO and Hamas, the only solution will be the total and complete annihilation of the state of Israel. One thing is clear from history: If Muslims stop terrorizing Jews there won't be anymore conflict. If Jews stop defending themselves against Muslim terror there won't be any more Jews.

The scattering of the Jews from the land and their present return is comparable to death and resurrection. Anti-Jewish Replacement Theology allows for Jewish death and burial but never resurrection. For Christians who hold to Replacement Theology, it is unthinkable that a Jewish state was ever born in 1948.

The most incredible line in this letter to the President is this one: "Perhaps the best way we can bless Israel is to encourage her to remember, as she deals with her neighbor Palestinians, the profound teaching on justice that the Hebrew prophets proclaimed so forcefully as an inestimably precious gift to the whole world." This statement is akin to giving a lecture about justice and kindness to the Polish Jews who chose to defend themselves against Nazi slaughter in the Polish ghetto. This statement places the terrorist (we are speaking of Palestinian terrorists—not Palestinian people in general) on the same moral equivalency as the terrorized. The same kind of argument came from churchmen during the Holocaust. They believed the Nazi propaganda that the Jews were responsible for the war and for the financial problems in Germany. These German church leaders encouraged Jews to accept whatever terror the Nazis cast upon them because it was their just recompense for all of the problems they were causing in Europe. The names of the leaders who signed this letter to the President and the large evangelical organizations they represent were published along with their letter in the *New York Times*. Here are the names as they appeared in the *Times*:

- Ronald J. Sider, President, Evangelicals for Social Action
- Don Argue, President, Northwest University
- Raymond J. Bakke, Chancellor, Bakke Graduate University
- Gary M. Benedict, President, The Christian and Missionary Alliance
- George K. Brushaber, President, Bethel University
- Gary M. Burge, Professor, Wheaton College and Graduate School
- Tony Campolo, President/Founder, Evangelical Association for the Promotion of Education
- Christopher J. Doyle, CEO, American Leprosy Mission
- Leighton Ford, President, Leighton Ford Ministries
- Daniel Grothe, Pastoral Staff, New Life Church, Colorado Springs
- Vernon Grounds, Chancellor, Denver Seminary
- Stephen Hayner, former President, InterVarsity Christian Fellowship
- Joel Hunter, Senior Pastor, Northland Church (Member, Executive Committee of the National Association of Evangelicals)
- Jo Anne Lyon, Founder/CEO, World Hope International
- Gordon MacDonald, Chair of the Board, World Relief
- Albert G. Miller, Professor, Oberlin College
- Richard Mouw, President, Fuller Theological Seminary
- David Neff, Editor, Christianity Today

- Glenn R. Palmberg, President, Evangelical Covenant Church
- Earl Palmer, Senior Pastor, University Presbyterian Church, Seattle
- Victor D. Pentz, Pastor, Peachtree Presbyterian Church, Atlanta
- John Perkins, President, John M. Perkins Foundation for Reconciliation and Development
- Bob Roberts, Jr., Senior Pastor, Northwood Church, Dallas
- Leonard Rogers, Executive Director Evangelicals for Middle East Understanding
- Andrew Ryskamp, Executive Director Christian Reformed World Relief Committee
- Chris Seiple, President, Institute for Global Engagement
- Robert A. Seiple, Former Ambassador-at-Large, International Religious Freedom U.S. State Department
- Luci N. Shaw, Author, Lecturer, Regent College, Vancouver
- Jim Skillen, Executive Director, Center for Public Justice
- Glen Harold Stassen, Professor, Fuller Theological Seminary
- Richard Stearns, President, World Vision
- Clyde D. Taylor, Former Chair of the Board, World Relief
- Harold Vogelaar, Director, Center of Christian-Muslim Engagement for Peace and Justice
- Berten Waggoner, National Director, Vineyard USA

One of the signers of this letter is a New Testament professor at Billy Graham's alma mater—Wheaton College. His name is Dr. Gary Burge. His book *Whose Land? Whose Promise?* plunges the reader into the abyss of Replacement Theology. Shockingly, this book, filled with bias against Jewish people, won the "Award of Merit" from the voice of Evangelicalism—Christianity Today. According to journalist Dexter Van Zile, reporter for the Committee for Accuracy in Middle East Reporting in America (CAMERA),

the book is a compellation of factual errors, misstatements, omissions and distortions that portray the modern state of Israel in an inaccurate manner. The errors are egregious and numerous. For example:

1. *Rev. Dr. Burge falsely stated that Israeli-Arabs are denied membership in Israel's labor movement, when in fact, one of the books he cites reports that Israeli-Arabs have been allowed full membership in Israel's largest union—the Histadrut—since 1959.*

2. *Rev. Dr. Burge falsely reported that Israeli-Arabs are prohibited from joining Israel's major political parties.*

3. *Rev. Dr. Burge mis-characterized UN Resolution 242 as requiring Israeli withdrawal to its "pre-1967 borders" when in fact it does not.*

4. *Rev. Dr. Burge portrays Hezbollah as a "resistance organization" when in fact its political agenda and leaders clearly state the organization is dedicated to the destruction of Israel—a fact he omits in his description.*

5. *Rev. Dr. Burge portrays the founding of the PLO as an attempt to resolve the problem of Palestinian refugees created by the 1948 war when in fact its founding was motivated by a desire for the destruction of Israel.*

In short, Burge's book is not an honest assessment of Israeli policies, but an inaccurate indictment.[3]

The front cover of the book shows the magnitude of Dr. Burge's opinion of the nation of Israel. Pictured is a massive Israeli tank bearing down on a small Palestinian child preparing to throw a rock in the tank's direction. Israel is portrayed as the vanquisher and the Arabs as the vanquished. The Arab boy is innocent David fighting evil Jewish Goliath. The book is a frightening example of Evangelicalism's new fondness for anti-Israel sentiments. Dr. Burge himself is part of a growing anti-Judaic Christian movement that opposes the modern state of Israel. Dr. Burge serves as a member of the advisory board to the Holy Land Christian Ecumenical Foundation and as president of Evangelicals for Middle East Understanding—an organization committed to Replacement Theology. He regularly speaks at Christian gatherings that question the land covenant God made with Abraham. One such gathering was the 2004 Friends of Sabeel—North America conference (Sabeel is a Replacement

Theology outpost based in Jerusalem). During this Christian conference, committed to dividing the Holy Land, a special guest of
honor listened intently as Dr. Burge and other evangelical leaders
spoke. The special guest? The terrorist Yasser Arafat. Dr. Burge
states: "From 1971 until 1982, the Palestine Liberation Organization (PLO) was based in Lebanon and waged numerous conflicts
with Israel in an attempt to redress the refugee problem"[4] But, did
the terrorist Yasser Arafat establish the PLO in order to help refugees? Actually, the PLO was founded for one main purpose: "The
elimination of Zionism in Palestine."[5] Somehow, Dr. Burge over-
looks this.

A landmark book that offers a serious challenge to the rising tide
of Replacement Theology within Evangelicalism in America has
been written by Dr. Barry E. Horner and it is called: *Future Israel: Why
Christian Anti-Judaism Must be Challenged.* In speaking of Gary Burge's
book, *Whose Land? Whose Promise?*, Dr. Horner states: "Gary Burge,
professor of NT at Wheaton College Graduate School, has aligned
himself with the pro-Palestinian and anti-Judaic movement that vo-
ciferously opposes the modern State of Israel, derided as unjust, carnal
Zionism...While the style is temperate, the overall thrust is uncom-
promisingly supercessionist, anti-Judaic, and pro-Palestinian."[6]

Dr. Horner shows the true heart of Replacement Theology and
its unquestioned commitment to reject the covenant God made
with Abraham:

*An especially egregious example of how this principle of nullification
of the Abrahamic covenant plays out in Burge's supercessionism concerns
his questioning of Father George Makhlouf, a parish priest of St. George's
Greek Orthodox Church in Ramallah, Israel: "I asked... 'How can you
argue with the Israeli claim to own this land since God gave it to the Jews
in the Old Testament? Israeli Jews have inherited the promises to Abraham, have they not?'... 'The church is actually the new Israel. What
Abraham was promised, Christians now possess because they are Abraham's true spiritual children just as the New Testament teaches.'" Burge
then makes a most revealing comment that appears to be utterly void of
a sense of church history, warts and all. "The Greek Orthodox tradition*

of Father George has been consistent in defending this view throughout the centuries. From the earliest years, the Middle Eastern churches have claimed the promises of the Old Testament for their own. This concept shows up in Orthodox icons. Churches display beautiful pictures (or icons) of Old Testament stories whose truths have now been swept up by the Christian tradition and 'baptized' with new meaning." What fails to be acknowledged here, in all its shameful ugliness, is that this "sweeping" process involved an Augustinian anti-Judaic heritage that later enveloped both the eastern church and the western church. Such an appeal to church tradition here, as if this might provide added weight of argument, only heightens the degree of disgrace caused by this supercessionist tradition that flowed through subsequent centuries.[7]

Dr. Horner also points out that Gary Burge suggests Jews have been disinherited by God forever from the land of Israel and His blessings because of their transgressions:

He strongly suggests that for these repeated transgressions, Israel has been disinherited from its blessings while the Christian church has inherited these same essential blessings by way of supercession or transference. The only problem here is that so many other passages in the OT promise God's ultimate triumph through grace, over Israel's sins, even as is the case in the saving of any sinner. So Burge either ignores or minimizes or relegates to past fulfillment these Bible passages. Consider the following Scriptural references that are said to condemn the nation of Israel's present ungodliness, causing it permanently to have become person non grata in God's sight:

Deut. 4:25–27 – yet reference to vv. 28–31 is omitted

Deut. 8:17–19 – yet reference to 30:1–14 (esp. vs. 6) is omitted

Isa. 1:16–17; 5:1–7 – yet references to 2:2–4; 11:1–16; 27:2–13; 35:1–10; 41:8–16; 43:1–7; 49:14–26; 62:1–5 are omitted

Jer. 3:19–20; 7:5–7 – yet references to 30:1–31:40; 33:1–26; Ezekiel 36–37 are omitted

Hos. 9:2–3 – yet references to 3:4–5; 11:8–11; 14:1–17 are omitted

Amos 4:1–2 – yet reference to 9:11–15 is omitted

Micah 2:1–3 – yet references to 4:1–8; 7:7–20 are omitted

The reader is strongly encouraged to read the additional references included here that Burge does not draw attention to in the main. Time after time they indicate the triumph of sovereign grace over the sins of Israel, even as Paul describes with regard to the Christian in Romans 5:20. Yes, the sins of Israel bring severe punishment, but not covenantal abandonment.[8]

Let's listen to Dr. Burge in his own words: "But the most important critique—and here I think we discover the Achilles' heel—is that Christian Zionism is committed to what I term a 'territorial religion.' It assumes that God's interests are focused on a land, a locale, a place."[9]

There is No Assumption in Promise

Notice the last sentence of this statement by Dr. Burge: "It assumes that God's interests are focused on a land, a locale, a place." Is it a blind assumption that God is jealous over Zion? Was the covenant God made with Abraham and confirmed with an oath just an assumption on Abraham's part? In this one line you can see the depth of error in Replacement Theology. There is no assumption in promise. When God makes a covenant it is unbreakable. We can never assume that it will be broken! Dr. Burge goes on to say: "From a New Testament perspective, the land is holy by reference to what transpired there in history. But it no longer has an intrinsic part to play in God's program for the world."[10]

Is this accurate? The land of Israel no longer has an intrinsic part to play in God's program for the world? Would the second coming of Jesus the Jewish Messiah have anything to do with God's program for the world? The Jewish Messiah is not returning to New York or Los Angeles. In fact, He is touching His feet upon the Mount of Olives which is in Jerusalem—the City of David—located geographically in a land, a locale, and place called Israel. Actually, it is impossible to discuss God's program for the world without talking about the land of Israel. One thinking otherwise would have to be persuaded by a 1,900-year-old theology that demands and insists that God has forgotten the Jews and His covenant with them.

Dr. Burge seems to indicate that the PLO's claim that they own the land carries more weight than God's Word. In defending Palestinian claims to the land He states in the preface to his book: "Does such a claim from the Bible trump a claim to historic residence?"[11] Dr. Burge allows for the Bible to be overruled by Palestinian claims because based on His Replacement Theology, God's covenant with Abraham has been redefined: "Christ is the reality behind all earthbound promises…land is rejected as the aim of faith; ….land is spiritualized as meaning something else;…the promise is historicized in Jesus, a man who lives in the land…Whatever the 'land' meant in the Old Testament, whatever the promise contained, this now belongs to Christians…The land was a metaphor, a symbol of a greater place beyond the soil of Canaan."[12]

Has God given us the right to change a promised piece of actual real estate into something ethereal, metaphorical, and spiritual? The very title of Dr. Burge's book, *Whose Land? Whose Promise?*, calls into question the validity of God's covenant with Abraham. Dr. Burge tells us the answer to the question "Who owns the land?" is not an easy one: "The answer is not just a matter of pointing to the promises of Abraham, identifying modern Israel as heirs to those promises, and then theologically justifying the Israeli land claim. On the contrary, Christian theology demands that the true recipients of these promises will be found in the Christian church. Perhaps the church alone receives these promises!"[13]

The core of Replacement Theology is found in these words of Dr. Burge: "Perhaps the church alone receives these promises!" Dr. Burge argues that Christians are actually the rightful owners of the land because under the New Covenant in Christ the promises to the Jews were removed. But, if the land according to Dr. Burge is now "spiritualized" and serves only as a "metaphor of a greater place beyond the land of Canaan" why would he spend time promoting the rights of Arabs to own the land? If the land according to

Dr. Burge no longer plays an intrinsic role in God's program for the world, why is he demanding it be divided? If God's interests are not in a "land, a locale, and a place" then why are Dr. Burge and other supercessionists pressuring the Jews to give the land to the Arabs? By saying that the "church alone receives these promises" Dr. Burge unveils the heart of Supercessionism: To the Jew, the land is only a metaphor of what they once had, and to the Arab an actual land, locale, and place. It's almost as if he is saying, "Anyone can occupy this land—anyone except Jews."

A Frightening Use of Metaphor

In fact, Dr. Burge goes so far as to say that non-Christian Israeli Jews have no land rights. Based on his interpretation of John chapter 15, Jews only have a right to stay in the land if they are born-again Christians. Burge writes: "The people of Israel cannot claim to be planted as vines in the land; they cannot be rooted in the vineyard unless first they are grafted into Jesus. Branches that attempt living in the land, the vineyard, which refuse to be attached to Jesus will be cast out and burned" (15:6).[14] Does this line sound familiar? This could be a quote from any anti-Semitic tirade from John Chrysostom to Martin Luther. If Israeli Jews do not convert to Christianity, are we to take Burge's suggestion and (metaphorically) cast them into the flames and burn them?

What is so concerning about Dr. Burge's use of John 15:6 is that this same Scripture was used during the Spanish Inquisition to justify driving Jews from their homes and land and then burning them at the stake. Rather than being embarrassed over the perversion of John 15:6 by the inquisitors, Dr. Burge unashamedly applies it to the expulsion of Jews from their land once again. If a passage like John 15:6 has been historically misinterpreted by inhumane and depraved Christian anti-Semites, why would someone use the same passage to deny Jews the right to their own land today? Have Christian leaders today forgotten the murderous violence unleashed upon Jews by baptized Christians in the Inquisition, crusades, pogroms, and ultimately in the Holocaust? Are we repeating the sins of our Christian ancestors?

Historically, many Christians have concluded that a good Jew is either a dead Jew or a Christian. In his book, *The Destruction of the European Jews*, Raul Hilberg writes: "The missionaries of Christianity had said in effect: You have no right to live among us as Jews. The secular rulers who followed had complained: You have no right to live among us. The German Nazis at last decreed: You have no right to live...The process began with the attempt to drive the Jews into Christianity. The development was continued in order to force the victims into exile. It was finished when the Jews were driven to their deaths."[15]

This same line of reasoning is being used once again by churchmen to drive Jews from the land of Israel. That an evangelical graduate school professor would call for the "burning" of Israeli Jews if they fail to convert to Christianity is frightening. Yes, Dr. Burge is using a biblical metaphor to strengthen his point but after the burning and gassing of millions of Jews during the Holocaust this harsh language is more than insensitive. Ultimately, he is saying that if Jews do not convert they must leave their land and homes. These same words have been used over the centuries by Christian leaders to drive Jews out of their communities. Actually, a pogrom (the ransacking of Jewish villages that ended in expulsion) was a preferable penalty for refusing baptism. Often, a failure to convert to Christianity was punishable by death through burning. When Christian leaders begin to use metaphorical words like "burning" in describing just punishment against Jews who do not convert to Christianity, it is not long before the metaphor becomes reality. The fact that a book of this nature won the "Award of Merit" from the flagship publication of Evangelicalism—Christianity Today—speaks volumes about the heart of American Christianity.

It is impossible to be anti-Israel without being anti-Jewish. To conclude that Jews do not have a right to live within the land of Israel without first being converted to Christianity denies this people a right to self-determination within their own land. The land of

Israel is so interwoven within the soul of the worldwide community of Jewish people that you cannot separate the two. If you deny the Jews their own land, you are in fact denying the Jews as a people. To be anti-Israel is to be anti-Jewish.

There are other Replacement theologians who are strongly influencing American Evangelicalism. Albertus Pieters (1897–1987) was professor of Bible and missions at Western Theological Seminary in Holland, Michigan. His theological works are highly regarded in the replacement movement today. Here is what he has to say concerning Jews:

God willed that after the institution of the New Covenant there should no longer be any Jewish people in the world—yet here they are! That is a fact—a very sad fact, brought about by their wicked rebellion against God....But is it not monstrous to hold that by reason of this wickedness the said undesired and undesirable group are now heirs to the many exceedingly precious promises of God? Shall we be accused of anti-Semitism, because we speak thus of the Jews? ....How is it possible to believe that there are still prophecies of divine grace to be fulfilled in a group upon which the wrath of God has come "to the uttermost"? ....Ignorant that their separateness from the rest of the world was in the divine purpose temporary, they strove to render it permanent. Thus that which had been in itself good and holy became through their error a source of poison in the life of the world; and "the Jew" became the great persistent international problem.[16]

Another evangelical leader with strong anti-Jewish leanings is O. Palmer Robertson, Visiting Professor at Knox Theological Seminary. Here is what he has to say about Jews in his recently published book, The Israel of God—Yesterday, Today, and Tomorrow:

(Jesus) is not, as some suppose, replacing Israel with the church. But He is reconstituting Israel in a way that makes it suitable for the new covenant. From this point on, it is not that the church takes the place of Israel, but that a renewed Israel of God is being formed by the shaping of the church. This kingdom will reach beyond the limits of the Israel of the *old covenant...The solemn consequences of this rejection find expression in the words of Jesus: "The kingdom shall be taken away from you and given to a people bearing the fruit of it" (Matt. 21:43). Israel as a nation would no more be able to claim that they possessed the kingdom of God in a way that was distinct from other nations. Yet the people of the new covenant would still be designated as Israel, "the Israel of God." This new covenant people would be formed around the core of twelve Israelites who were chosen to constitute the ongoing Israel of God.*[17]

In his book, *Future Israel*, Barry Horner comments on Robertson's conclusions: "This is not reconstitution; it is the prodigal son attempting to disinherit the elder brother and claim his title. To suggest that old Israel, having Jewish individuality, nationality, and territory is 'reconstituted' so that the original distinctive Jewishness is reformed but not replaced, is to play with words while at the same time retaining an eliminationist agenda. It is to subtly deal with the 'Jewish problem,' even as Napoleon suggested, through 'the abolition of Jewry by dissolving it into Christianity.'"[18]

How Should We Respond?

What is our response to the anti-Semitism within Christian history? What are we responsible to do in this hour? Will we be silent spectators? Will we be just another indifferent face in the window? The revolution of separation is here in full force. This book serves as a warning of what is about to come. Will we acknowledge God's choice of the Jewish people? Will we be loyal to His call to minister to them in this hour? Will we have understanding of the times and embrace the revolution of separation—intentionally standing with the believing Jews within the household of faith as one new man and together embracing the Jewish people as a whole? To separate oneself for the ministry to Jews (according to Matthew 25) is to minister to Jesus. This is why such rich blessing is appointed to the person who is loyal to God's Word in this matter.

As more and more Christian leaders separate themselves from the Jewish people and lead a charge against the chosen, the Lord is doing something incredible in the earth. He is sending a revolution of restoration. Even now, Our Jewish Messiah, Jesus, is restoring the age long broken relationship between Christian Gentiles and Jews—especially those Jews who are in the household of faith. In our next section on restoration we will see that our families, our churches, and the world harvest of souls depends on whether or not we embrace the coming revolution of restoration. We have made it through the difficult first half of this book. The second half describes the redemptive restoration you will experience when the age long divide between Jews and Gentiles is healed. Our first stop will be in the city of Radom, Poland, where a resurrection of sorts occurred in the summer of 2008.

PART II:

The Revolution of Restoration

*I think we do not attach sufficient importance
to the restoration of the Jews. We do not think
enough of it. But certainly, if there is anything
promised in the Bible it is this.*

Charles Spurgeon

In the summer of 2008 in the Polish city of Radom between Lublin and Lodz, a crime was uncovered. After sixty four years of lying still in their earthen grave, nearly one hundred witnesses rose again to testify. They were buried side by side, and, if it wasn't for the Radom construction workers building a new road, they may have never been found. When the witnesses stood upright again after their long burial, each gave testimony to the day they were born and the day they died. Surprisingly, each witness was very well preserved—their faces still showing color and hue. These Polish road workers uncovered the largest single find of Jewish gravestones in recent memory. Artistically decorated and painted, this archeological discovery holds deep significance for the few remaining Jews living in Poland.

Before the Holocaust there were 3.3 million Polish Jews. After the Holocaust there were only three hundred thousand. Because of fierce post war anti-Semitism, many of the survivors fled the country. After Hitler was dead and the Third Reich defeated, Jews continued to be slaughtered by baptized Christians in Poland. The hatred ran deep. Today, the contemporary Jewish population in Poland numbers between eight and twelve thousand—a mere whisper of the 3.3 million prior to the gas chambers and the pogroms.

What were the gravestones doing buried horizontally side by side in the earth? After the Jewish community had been deported from cities across Poland, Polish Christians desecrated Jewish graves. Over the years, as the Christian cemeteries filled up, the boundary lines separating Jewish and gentile burial grounds were erased. When it came time to bury a Christian saint the Jew was exhumed and discarded and his grave was given to the Gentile. Even in death the Jews were dispossessed of their last remaining inheritance. What was the difference? There were few (if any) remaining Jews to visit the cemetery anyway, right? Over time, Christians not only confiscated the graves of Jews but found that the well constructed grave stones came in handy for paving roads. That's where the road workers in Radom found them—lying in the quiet stillness of a long forgotten road, over grown with grass and weeds—an old detour perhaps? If you stroll through any given city in Poland today, at some point you will probably walk on the hollowed, silent names of your elder Jewish brothers and sisters—unaware.

Roads. Christianity has been paved with the bones of dead Jews and has trampled underfoot their last remaining dignity. Burying Jewish gravestones was the final attempt to remove any flickering evidence of Jewish existence. Yet, supernaturally the candle of the Jewish people is burning brightly once again. They are indeed coming up out of the valley of dry bones—never to be buried in some forgotten roadway again.

Thankfully, this trampling underfoot is coming to an end. A righteous remnant of gentile believers is being awakened by the Holy Spirit in this hour. In chapter 9 we will read the heroic story of Le Chambon-Sur-Lignon—a village of French Huguenot Christians who rescued over five thousand Jewish men, women, and children during the Holocaust. There are many such heroic stories of godly gentile saints who have shown kindness and mercy to Jews throughout the ages. Yes, the false church will continue to pave its pathway with dispossessed Jewish property, promises, and covenants. But, among righteous believers a revolution of restoration is on the horizon. Even now, a full scale revolution of restoration is reconciling gentile believers to their Jewish heritage. The nourishing sap of the olive tree—the spiritual commonwealth of Israel, is once again flowing through gentile veins. What can we expect the Lord to do as this new revolution of restoration approaches? Does our life and future depend on embracing this powerful revolution? What's really at stake here? What are the implications of being restored to our

Hebraic heritage? How will the revolution of restoration affect our families, our churches, and our world?

The two minute warning bell has sounded. Like never before it is time to embrace God's eternal plan for the ages. Time is short. A revolution of restoration is fast approaching—embrace it. God is restoring Israel—His covenant people. But, without you the restoration cannot be completed. The church plays a central role in Israel's restoration. In the following three chapters: "Roads," "Roots," and "The Olive Tree," we will see how the future success of our families, our churches, and the world harvest of souls is dependant on whether or not we embrace the coming revolution of restoration and build a roadway back to our Hebraic beginnings.

Roads

The prophet Isaiah has something significant to say about roads: "Go through, go through the gates! Build up, build up the highway! Take out the stones, lift up a banner for the peoples!" (Isa. 62:10). For nearly 1,900 years the Christian church has been building a detour away from our Hebraic foundation. In order to erase the fact that we are rooted in Israel's covenants, we have resorted to such things as using Jewish gravestones as asphalt just to prove our point. If we choose to be involved in building a road of reconciliation back to our beginnings, where would we start? When God first made His covenant with Abraham this is what He said: "Now the Lord had said to Abram: 'Get out of your country, from your family and from your father's house, to a land that I will show you. I will make you a great nation; I will bless you and make your name great; and you shall be a blessing. I will bless those who bless you, and I will curse him who curses you; and in you all the families of the earth shall be blessed'" (Gen. 12:1–3).

Through Abraham's family all the families of the earth would be blessed. Through his family came the covenants and the promises: "....the Israelites, to whom pertain the adoption, the glory, the covenants, the giving of the law, the service of God, and the promises; of whom are the fathers and from whom, according to the flesh, Christ came" (Rom. 9:4–5).

Even salvation would come through Abraham's family. Jesus said in John 4:22: "Salvation is of the Jews." The starting point with God has always been the family. If we are going to rebuild a roadway to our Hebraic heritage the family is an appropriate starting point.

The Christian pollster George Barna tells us that among evangelical Christians the rate of divorce stands at thirty-three percent.[1] Other statistics about the Christian home are staggering as well: teenage pregnancy, sexually transmitted diseases, and large numbers of Christian college students who are rejecting the faith of their parents (eighty to ninety percent)—just to name a few. Are we missing something? As we have already read, Paul the Jewish apostle says in Ephesians 2:

"Therefore remember that you, once Gentiles in the flesh—who are called the Uncircumcision by what is called the Circumcision made in the flesh by hands—that at that time you were without Christ, being aliens from the commonwealth of Israel and strangers form the covenants of promise, having no hope and without God in the world. But now in Christ Jesus you who once were far off have been brought near by the blood of Christ" (Eph. 2:11–13).

Paul is saying that when Gentiles came to Christ they also entered into the "commonwealth" or the "national life" of Israel. Are there certain customs and practices in the national life of Israel that the gentile church has rejected—thus seriously weakening and wounding family life and structure? We believe so. If we are to restore a roadway of health and wholeness in our families the following paving stones are of wonderful use. When it comes to family life there are many things we can learn from our Jewish elders. Here are just a few:

The Jewish Concept of Love and Marriage

When a Jewish couple is married under the wedding canopy or "chuppa" they believe that they are entering into a covenant relationship that will last throughout their shared lifetime. To them, the white canopy represents the glory cloud that descended upon Mount Sinai when Moses and the children of Israel entered into covenant with God. Inscribed within the wedding rings of Jewish couples are the Hebrew words: "Dodi Li Va-ani lo." These words come from Song of Songs 2:16: "My beloved is mine, and I am his." Jewish couples use these words to express their mutual respect for one another. In the Jewish understanding of marriage, the husband and wife are equals in strength and power. They have been joined together by God Himself. Dr. Marvin Wilson, in his outstanding book, *Our Father Abraham*, has this to say about the Jewish concept of marriage:

One of the vital functions of marriage is to complement (not to compete with) one's spouse. Genesis 2:18, 20 states that the woman is created to be ezer kenegdo. R. David Freedman has pointed out that the word ezer, often translated "helper," actually means "power" (or "strength"), as demonstrated by its use elsewhere in the Hebrew Bible. Furthermore, he takes kenegdo, an expression rendered "suitable" for him (NIV), as meaning one "equal to him," a rendering based on later Mishnaic Hebrew. Thus, when God says, he will make a "helper suitable for him (i.e., the man)," he likely means that a woman is a power equal to a man; she is his match; she corresponds to him in every way. Indeed, "woman was not intended to be merely man's helper. She was to be instead his partner." Man and woman are symbolically matched to one another in mutually dependent relationship—hence the expression "one flesh" (Gen. 2:24).[2]

A Cold Bowl of Soup

Today, for the most part, the Hebraic concept of love and marriage is not taught to Christian couples who are preparing for marriage. In the Western world, a high value is placed on the romantic feelings we have toward the one we are to marry. But this goes against the grain of Hebrew thought. Again, from Marvin Wilson:

For Hebrew men and women of Bible times, living in an Eastern society gave them a different perspective on love. To begin with, love was more a commitment than a feeling. It was seen foremost as a pledge rather than an emotional high. It was a person's good word to stick with someone, to make that relationship work; it was not merely a warm sensation inside. For centuries, Jewish people have pointed to one particular verse to illustrate the need for love to develop and deepen after marriage. The passage is Genesis 24:67: "Isaac brought her [Rebekah] into his mother, Sarah's, tent; and he took Rebekah and she became his wife, and he loved her." The text above says that after she became his wife, "he loved her." In short, for the Hebrew patriarchs, love came after marriage; it was not a matter of falling in love and then marrying. Thus, in the biblical world of the ancient Near East, couples were expected to grow to love each other after marriage. In the modern West, however, the emphasis has been more on marrying the person that you love rather than learning to love the one that you marry. Though both dimensions of love are important for modern Christian marriage, there remains a decisive lack of emphasis in Christian preaching, teaching, and literature about the need for love to blossom after the marriage ceremony.[3]

Jewish tradition teaches that marriage begins like a cold bowl of soup that grows hotter and hotter over a lifetime. In the West we teach that marriage begins with love and romance—a hot bowl of soup. Historically however, instead of growing hotter the soup grows colder over a lifetime. In his book, *The Jewish Way of Love and Marriage*, Maurice Lamm says:

The trouble with American marriage is our style of courtship. It is artificial, juvenile, and premature, and emphasizes romance, sex appeal, charm, and affluence to the exclusion of the deeper, more enduring aspects of character.....Romantic love is based on an idealized notion of the other person, which requires remoteness—psychological, physical, or social—to be maintained. Hence the inherent paradox: romantic love desires intimacy, but at the very moment of intimacy, love evaporates.... Most marriages are failures. Not because most marriages end in divorce, but because in most unions one or both partners are miserable. Most of marriage's ills, perhaps, can be traced to faulty selection of a spouse that was precipitated by a glorious moment, a flash of insight, or an uncontrollable passion[4]

Family as a Foundation Stone

Paul said that the Jewish people are our "fathers" (Rom. 9:5). Certainly, when it comes to the family there are some things we can learn from our spiritual fathers. Proverbs 22:28 says: "Do not remove the ancient landmark which your fathers have set." Sadly, when it comes to the Hebraic concept of love and marriage, the modern church has systematically pushed the envelope of the scriptural concept of marriage. Because the church for the most part has rejected her Hebraic roots, she no longer sees the traditional family through the eyes of a Jew. Marriage is now classified as a loving relationship between two human beings. Same sex marriage is now endorsed and sanctioned by several church denominations. Ministers are now ordained to the priesthood who are committed to same sex unions. Because divorce is so rampant in "Christian America," one third of the children born in the United States will be raised in one parent families. The hearts of the children (gentile believers) must be turned back to the fathers (the Jews). The following ominous words are the last words in the Old Testament: "And he will turn the hearts of the fathers to the children, and the hearts of the children to their fathers, lest I come and strike the earth with a curse" (Mal. 4:6). Could the failure of the family be a result of 1,900 years of moving the ancient landmarks our Jewish fathers have set?

As the family has disintegrated, we have looked for substitutes for the biblical guidelines that define a family as a husband, wife, and their children. We have gone so far as saying that it takes a village to raise a family in modern America. However, history proves that whenever a society discards the biblical definition of family, that society eventually crumbles in ruins. In the Hebrew mind, the "family is the quintessential foundation stone of the world—and marriage is the foundation of the family. When you marry, you find a lifelong, loving, and devoted friend. You grow together, emotionally, spiritually, in all possible ways. There is no substitute for a happy marriage."[5] The Hebrews have been promoting and practicing the principles of biblical marriage for nearly four thousand years. The family dates back to creation and when Adam and Eve were married. According to Jewish tradition, God was their best man. For the Jew, marriage is to be honored because it is holy. In fact, the Hebrew word *kadosh* is the word "holy" and is the root word of *kiddushin* which means "marriage." Thus, the very word marriage itself means "holy," a sobering thought to be sure. Could this be why we call marriage "holy matrimony?" In the Jewish mind, the oldest of all human institutions is the family. They view it as the bedrock of civilization. The late Rabbi Aryeh Kaplan wrote: "The family has always been the strength of Judaism. Indeed, Judaism may be able to survive without the synagogue, but it cannot survive without the family."[6]

Rabbi Stolper has said: "The Jewish family has long been a model of harmony, love and stability, the envy of the entire civilized world. The very social evils that tend to disrupt and destroy modern society, such as divorce, prostitution, adultery, wife-beating or juvenile delinquency, were until recent times almost unknown among traditional, unassimilated Jews. While observant Jews in America… have also been affected by this generation's tendency to solve marital problems through divorce, the difference in percentages still points to a qualitative difference of considerable weight."[7]

Listen to a few of the many Jewish sayings about love and marriage from the Jewish book of wit and wisdom:

Love turns one person into two and two into one. —Abarbanel

He who has no wife lives without joy, without blessings, and without good. —The Talmud

118

True love comes quietly, without banners or flashing lights. If you hear bells, get your ears checked.

If your wife is short, bend down and listen to her. —The Talmud

Set me as a seal on your heart, As a seal on your arm; For love is strong as death. —Song of songs

Hatred stirs up strife, but love covers all wrongs. —Proverbs

Even in Paradise, it's not good to be alone.

Love is not blind—it sees more, not less. But because it sees more, it is willing to see less. —Rabbi Julie Gordon

Love is sweet, but tastes better with bread. —Yiddish Proverb

A woman who is loved always has success.

Honor your wives that you may be enriched. —The Talmud

Forty days before an embryo is formed, a heavenly voice proclaims: the daughter of so-and-so will be the wife of so-and-so. —The Talmud

If you want to know about a man, you can find out an awful lot by looking at the woman he married.

All love that depends on some material cause and the material cause passes away, the love vanishes too; but if it does not depend on some material cause, it will never pass away. —Ethics of the Fathers

House and riches are an inheritance from fathers, but a prudent wife is from God. —Proverbs

An angry man sleeps alone.[8]

The Family Blessing

The road to wholeness in families is paved with blessing. The word blessing in Hebrew is *Bracha*. It carries the meaning of conferring praise upon another or to speak well of another. Though the Hebraic principle of blessing is a foreign concept in many Christian homes today, it was very familiar to the biblical Hebrews. The gospel of Mark records how mothers and fathers brought their children to Jesus to bless: "Then they brought little children to Him, that He might touch them; but the disciples rebuked those who brought them. But when Jesus saw it, He was greatly displeased and said to them, 'Let the little children come to Me, and do not forbid them; for of such is the kingdom of God. Assuredly, I say to you, whoever does not receive the kingdom of God as a little child will by no means enter it.' And He took them up in His arms, laid His hands on them, and blessed them" (Mark 10:13–16).

When Jesus was born, a verbal blessing was conferred upon Him. Likewise, He consistently conferred words of blessing upon others. One of the most poignant pictures of Jesus is at His ascension when He lifts His hands and blesses His disciples: "And He led them out as far as Bethany, and He lifted up His hands and blessed them. Now it came to pass, while He blessed them, that He was parted from them and carried up into heaven" (Luke 24:50–51).

The road we have built has veered away from the wisdom of our Hebraic fathers. Because we have not learned to bless, verbal abuse is now at epidemic levels in America. A family that curses rather than blesses passes those curses to the next generation. James says this about the dangers of a verbally abusive tongue:

Even so the tongue is a little member and boasts great things. See how great a forest a little fire kindles! And the tongue is a fire, a world of iniquity. The tongue is so set among our members that it defiles the whole body, and sets on fire the course of nature, and it is set on fire by hell..... no man can tame the tongue. It is an unruly evil, full of deadly poison. With it we bless our God and Father and with it we curse men, who

*have been made in the similitude of God. Out of the same mouth proceed
blessing and cursing. My brethren, these things ought not to be so* (James
3:5-6, 8-10).

Andrew Vachss is an attorney who has written extensively
about the destruction that verbal abuse is causing in families today.
Here is what he says about a family that has forgotten the principle
of blessing:

*Emotional abuse threatens to become a national illness. The emotion-
al abuse of children can lead, in adulthood, to addiction, rage, a severely
damaged sense of self and an inability to truly bond with others. Of all the
forms of child abuse, emotional abuse may be the cruelest and longest lasting of all. Emotional abuse is the systematic diminishment of another. It is
designed to reduce a child's self-concept to the point where the victim considers himself unworthy—unworthy of respect, unworthy of friendship,
unworthy of natural birthright of all children: love and protection.*

*Emotional abuse can be as deliberate as a gunshot: "You're fat.
You're stupid. You're ugly."*

*Emotional abuse can be active: "You'll never be the success your
brother was. I'm ashamed you're my son."*

*Emotional abuse conditions the child to expect abuse in later life.
Emotional abuse is a time bomb, but its effects are rarely visible, because
the emotionally abused tend to implode, turning the anger against themselves.*[9]

Friday evening is a strategic time for blessing in Jewish families.
In the Jewish calendar a day begins at sundown rather than sunup.
Thus, the Sabbath starts Friday evening at sundown. As the sun is
setting, the family is seated around the dining room table and the
mother opens the Sabbath by lighting two table candles. The first
candle represents the beginning and sanctification of the Sabbath as

a time of renewal and rest. The second candle represents the Exodus from Egypt because God brought the children of Israel out of darkness into light.

The father of the household will now read a portion from Proverbs 31 and verbally bless his wife in front of the family: "Many daughters have done well, but you excel them all. Charm is deceitful and beauty is passing, but a woman who fears the Lord, she shall be praised. Give her the fruit of her hands, and let her own works praise her in the gates" (Prov. 31:29–31).

The children will now bless their mother according to Proverbs 31:28: "Her children rise up and call her blessed." After the mother has been blessed she now reads a portion from Psalm 112 and blesses her husband: "Praise the Lord! Blessed is the man who fears the Lord, who delights greatly in His commandments. His descendant will be mighty on earth; the generation of the upright will be blessed. Wealth and riches will be in his house, and his righteousness endures forever. Unto the upright there arises light in the darkness; He is gracious, and full of compassion, and righteous. A good man deals graciously and lends; He will guide his affairs with discretion. Surely he will never be shaken" (Ps. 112:1–6).

After the father and mother bless each other, the father will rise and bless his children. King David did this after leading the processional of the ark of the covenant into the city of Jerusalem: "Then David returned to bless his household" (2 Sam. 6:20). The words that the fathers speak over their children are actually the words that Jacob used to bless his two grandsons Ephraim and Manasseh. While Joseph served in Egypt, born to him were two sons: "Joseph called the name of the firstborn Manasseh: 'For God has made me forget all my toil and all my father's house.' And the name of the second he called Ephraim: 'For God has caused me to be fruitful in the land of my affliction'" (Gen. 41:51–52). Thus, Manasseh means "forgetfulness" and Ephraim means "fruitfulness."

Later on when Joseph was reunited with his father Jacob, Jacob laid his hands on the two boys and spoke a blessing: "By you

Israel will bless, saying, 'May God make you as Ephraim and as Manasseh!'" (Gen. 48:20). Jacob was actually saying: "From this day forward all of Israel will bless their children by making this declaration over them: 'May you forget the pain of your past (Manasseh) and may you be fruitful in your future (Ephraim).'" This blessing of Ephraim and Manasseh has been proclaimed over children in Jewish homes around the world every Friday evening until this day. Is it any wonder that Jewish people are so fruitful?

Often, mothers will add a blessing over their daughters: "The Lord make the woman who is coming to your house like Rachel and Lea, the two who built the house of Israel; and may you prosper in Ephrathah and be famous in Bethlehem" (Ruth 4:11).

The biblical precedent of blessing children became "a natural part of Jewish life; it included a warm and loving embrace; it required the laying on of hands; the person giving the blessing shared his spiritual heritage; the blessing included words of increase and expansion; the person blessing required a degree of spiritual discernment; the blessing was spoken; and it required bold faith to bring results."[10]

After the entire family has received words of affirmation from the Scriptures, the father will then give thanks for the wine and bread: For the wine, "Blessed art Thou oh Lord God, King of the universe who brings forth the fruit of the vine." For the bread, "Blessed art Thou oh Lord God, King of the universe who brings forth bread from the earth." A wonderful Sabbath meal is now served on the family's best china.

The day of rest and renewal is underway and the Jewish family will remain together until Saturday evening at sundown. At that time, a closing Sabbath meal will be shared together as a family. During the Sabbath the family will have enjoyed three hearty meals together, lots of singing, humor, games, and much laughter.

During the Middle Ages, it was believed that if the synagogues were destroyed (which they were through fire and plunder) then the faith of the Jews would effectively be destroyed. However, there was a serious miscalculation in this theory: The faith of Jews is not based in the synagogue—it is based in the home. The father and mother in a Jewish home accept the biblical mandate to train their children spiritually within the context of the household.

For centuries, Christianity has rejected the Hebraic concept that the center of the faith communities life and learning is in the home. Rather, we have taught that the church building is the central place where learning occurs. When Jewish families are enjoying a family time of blessing and prayer on Friday evenings where are Christian families? To be honest, we are generally in the theater, the mall, or a sports event. Our families are scattered and separated in different Friday evening events of one kind or another. Because Christian families do not always bless, pray, or enjoy a mealtime together, the family unit has been weakened. Do you suppose it is because we have forgotten our Hebraic roots? George Barna, President of the Christian based Barna Research Group has surveyed Christian families about their spiritual life together. His findings are shocking:

Our national surveys have shown that while more than 4 out of 5 parents (85 percent) believe they have the primary responsibility for the moral spiritual development of their children, more than two out of three of them abdicate that responsibility to their church. Their virtual abandonment of leading their children spiritually is evident in how infrequently they engage in faith-oriented activities with their young ones. For instance, we discovered that in a typical week, fewer than 10 percent of parents who regularly attend church with their kids read the Bible together, pray together (other than at meal times) or participate in an act of service as a family unit. Even fewer families—1 out of every 20—have any type of worship experience together with their kids, other than while they are at church during a typical month.

In short, most families do not have a genuine spiritual life together. However, we also found that this is not disturbing to most of them for two reasons. First, they are merely following the precedent that was set for them. In other words, American parents—even those who are born-again churchgoers described by their church as "pillars"—are generally doing what their parents did with them: dropping off the kiddies at church and allowing the religious professionals to mastermind the spiritual development of the young people. No matter how much church leaders preach about the need for parents to personally invest in the spiritual growth of children, adults tend to revert to what was modeled for them, noting that carting the kids to church and occasional religious events is sufficient. *"After all,"* explained one mother, echoing a sentiment that has become a very common reply emerging from our research, *"that's what my parents did with me and I turned out pretty good."* This notion of turning out *"pretty good"* is especially widespread among baby boomers.

Second, most churchgoing parents are neither spiritually mature nor spiritually inclined and, therefore, they do not have a sense of urgency or necessity about raising their kids to be spiritual champions.[11]

Peaceful Sabbath

The common greeting on the Sabbath day is *Shabbat shalom* which means "peaceful Sabbath." A major Hebraic concept of the home is *Shalom bayit*—"a peaceful home." The Sabbath is a day in which the family enters into a time of spiritual and physical renewal and Jews live the first six days of the work week in wonderful expectation of its arrival. If you have ever traveled to Israel, one major thing you will take away is the peace and holiness still found in a family day of renewal—the Sabbath. It is never too late to exit the detour that has led to the present deterioration of the family. It was Replacement Theology that inspired the church to jealously reject her Hebraic roots—especially those that benefit the family. Even the Sabbath has been rejected. The argument has been that we are under grace not law. Therefore, the Sabbath has been done away with. Honoring the Sabbath as a day of rest and renewal for the family is one of the Ten Commandments. Have the other nine commands been nullified as well? Interestingly, you can find all of the Ten Commandments proclaimed in the New Testament—even the Sabbath commandment. Jesus said: "The Sabbath is made for man, not man for the Sabbath" (Mark 2:27). In other words, the Sabbath is given as a gift to man so that he might enjoy a day of rest and renewal.

Does this mean that gentile Christians are required to rest on the Sabbath? Speaking to the Colossians Paul says: "So let no one judge you in food or in drink, or regarding a festival or new moon or Sabbaths" (Col. 2:16). To the Romans Paul said: "One person esteems one day above another, another esteems every day alike. Let each be fully convinced in his own mind" (Rom. 14:5). Paul seems to be saying to gentile Christians that for them the Sabbath requirement has been relaxed. This does not however nullify the importance of a day of rest and renewal. In the past, the church honored Sunday as a day of rest and renewal. This has changed. Even Sunday has become a stressful day filled with consumerism and endless activity.

Our encouragement to you is to find a day of the week to rest. Sunday—the traditional Lord's day for the church is a wonderful day to worship, attend church and rest. By all means, spend the day with your family and enjoy a family meal together. Bless God for His provision and speak words of affirmation and blessing over your family. For those in ministry, Sunday is not a day of rest. If that is your situation, find another day of the week that suits your family—perhaps Saturday will work.

Family time takes planning, so prepare during the week what kinds of things you will do on your day of renewal. Enjoy God's creation. Go to the park. Watch a sunrise or sunset together. Eat, share, and pray together and make blessing God and each other central in your day. Try turning off cell phones, MP3s, computers, flat screen TVs, and simply enjoy one another. If this is not an established family pattern it will take some adjustment. Start slow. You cannot force this on your children. Be patient—pulling ourselves out of a 1,900-year-old rut will not be easy, but the benefits enjoyed from traveling on your new "Hebraic" road will be worth it. There are many resources available to help you plan a family meal from a Messianic Jewish perspective. Shabbat Shalom!

The Husband as Covering of the Home

Today, Christian wives are waiting for their husbands to lead the home spiritually. Because men in general have not been taught that their Hebraic heritage is to be the godly covering of their homes, families endure much suffering. The Proverbs 31 woman was a powerful leader in her community. What was one of the key elements of the success of this outstanding woman of God? Verse 28 gives us some initial insight: "Her children rise up and call her blessed; her husband also, and he praises her." The husband—fulfilling Hebraic tradition—had been consistently encouraging and teaching his children to honor both father and mother. In the Jewish home, the fifth commandment is vital for the homes survival. Paul refers to the fifth commandment in Ephesians 6:1–3:

"Children, obey your parents in the Lord, for this is right. 'Honor your father and mother,' which is the first commandment with promise: 'that it may be well with you and you may live long on the earth.' And you, fathers, do not provoke your children to wrath, but bring them up in the training and admonition of the Lord."

We see here that within the context of our Hebraic roots, the father was chiefly responsible to cover, lead, and train his children in the way of the Lord. As well, to breach the authority of father or mother was to breach the commandment of God to honor them. In fact, in a Hebraic context the main role of children was to respect and honor their parents. We have reversed this order in the Christian home. Today, the roles have been radically altered. It is now the duty of parents to honor and respect their children and to give to them all of the desires of their heart—or else! This is not biblical. As a result, rebellion, disobedience, haughtiness, and dishonor of parents are at an all time high in Christian homes.

The Proverbs 31 father taught his children to honor and respect both mother and father through personal example. He consistently blessed, praised, and honored his wife in their presence. By blessing his wife during the Sabbath meal the children learned the principle of giving honor where it was due.

The love and praise from her husband and the honor afforded to her from her children was not the only things that made this woman so fulfilled in life. Verse 31 gives us another insight: "Give her of the fruit of her hands, and let her own works praise her in the gates." The gates of an ancient Hebrew city were the place where the elders met to oversee the governing issues—city services, laws, property rights, etc. Basically the gates were a kind of city hall. How did this woman's success find so much praise in the gates? V. 23 tells us: "Her husband is known in the gates, when he sits among the elders of the land." This godly man not only blessed and praised his wife in front of his children, but he publicly praised her as well! He was an elder of the city himself. Can you imagine this man standing up in a meeting about the property redemption rights of a certain Benjamin or Samuel:

"Gentlemen, before we call this meeting to order I would like to praise my wife for the programs she has started in our community for the poor and needy (v. 20). I know that the entire city is talking about her concern for others, but I would like to add my own blessing and praise for my wife. She is gifted with wisdom and kindness (v. 26) and walks in the fear of the Lord (v. 30). I am very honored to be her husband, and I know our entire city is grateful for her leadership in our community."

It would have been unthinkable for this man of God to ever degrade or demean his wife privately and God forbid, publicly. He knew his own success in the community and within the home was dependent on the example of blessing he set for others—especially his children. Could the severe rebellion we are facing in Christian families today be a result of the absence of the spiritual covering of fathers? It's an endless cycle isn't it? Husbands neglect their duty to love and cover their wives. Unloved and shattered, wives in turn begin to disrespect their husbands. Rather than giving honor to one another as husband and wife, dishonor is expressed—all the while teaching the same example to the children. How can we as parents expect our children to bless and honor us if we fail to bless and honor each other?

In this chapter we have seen how centuries of building a detour away from our biblical Hebraic roots has weakened the Christian family. Traditional Hebraic concepts of love, marriage, family meals, verbal blessing, the home as the center of life and learning, spiritual leadership, honor, and respect have in many ways been forgotten. The two minute warning has sounded and righteous fathers and mothers the world over are now restoring the highway to the Hebraic roots of home life. It is now time to return to our biblical heritage concerning marriage and the family and recover all that has been lost.

For sixty-four years in the city of Radom, Poland, the burial markers of nearly one hundred Jews had been used as roadway pavement stones. Thankfully, due to the efforts of the Jewish historical society these markers have now been moved to their proper place in a Jewish cemetery. It's not too late to restore the ancient boundary markers to their proper location. Our spiritual fathers—the ancient Hebrews—set those markers in place and laid the foundation of a road that led to blessing, health, and wholeness for our families. Jeremiah the prophet spoke of these forgotten old roads: "Thus says the Lord: 'Stand in the ways and see, and ask for the old paths, where the good way is, and walk in it; then you will find rest for your souls'" (Jer. 6:16).

Roads. It is critical in this hour that we find this old Hebraic pathway and begin walking on it for the sake of our families. 1,900 years of detours have in many ways left us as weary wanderers. It's now time to return to the old path and the good way. In the process of return and restoration we will find rich meaning and rest for our souls.

Roots

We have no awareness of how anemic, loveless, narrow
predictable and mechanical a fellowship or people are that
have lost their identification with Israel. We do not understand
that the rudiments of the faith and its very root go deep into
the life of that people and that people's God...It is
enlarging and liberating to know that we have such an ancestry
and such a destiny as had been exclusively reserved for one
people alone, the Israel of God, into which now we have been
brought by the blood of the Messiah.
Art Katz

Two percent of the U.S. population—a total of six million people—have been adopted. If you include biological parents, adoptive parents and siblings, one in eight Americans are touched by
adoption. With the advent of the worldwide web and the relative
ease in gaining information, a large majority of adoptive children
are searching for their roots today. The experience can become an
amazing life adventure filled with emotional highs and lows. Adoptive children search for their roots for many reasons. Beyond basic

curiosity, one of the major reasons why people search for their fathers and mothers is for medical purposes. Nowadays it's standard to give your family medical history in preparation for even simple procedures—like annual physicals. Knowing the health history of your parents and siblings can be of critical importance if you ever face medical complications.

It's very important for the health and wholeness of the body of Christ that we discover the spiritual heritage of the family we have been engrafted into. Beyond basic curiosity, it's imperative today that we find our Hebraic roots because our spiritual wellness depends on it.

After centuries of wandering away from the Hebraic roots of our faith, the church now stands at a crossroads. To continue forging a path without the nourishing roots of our early beginnings will further drive a wedge between us and our calling. As a result, the church will never experience the fullness of God's glory, and will miss her end-time prophetic calling and destiny. The present hour demands our loyalty to God's Word. The lateness of the moment requires us to hear and obey the Word of God in the power of the Holy Spirit. It is time to return to the supporting root of the spiritual commonwealth of Israel.

In our last chapter we discovered the importance of returning to the biblical pattern of love and marriage, blessing and rest. These principles offer rich meaning and healing to our families. In this chapter we will see that Christianity itself can become truly authentic when it returns to its Hebraic heritage. The principles in this chapter offer rich meaning and healing to the body of Christ. As we look towards the final harvest and the reconciling of all things it is crucial that the church is restored to her original foundation.

Because of the erroneous doctrine of Replacement Theology that has been engrained in Christian thinking for ages, the church today has little awareness that it is actually a part of the spiritual commonwealth of Israel. Paul the apostle wrote his letter to gentile Ephesian believers in order to clear up their confusion about their origin. Listen again to a few points from Paul's message about Hebraic roots: "Therefore remember that you, once Gentiles in the flesh—who are called Uncircumcision by what is called the Circumcision made in the flesh by hands" (Eph. 2:11).

Cornelius

In the Jewish mind there were only two kinds of people in the world: circumcised Jews and uncircumcised Gentiles. To the Jew, a Gentile was an unbeliever and a person who was far removed from the covenants and promises of the God of the Hebrews. In fact, it was nearly fifteen years before the early Jewish believers were willing to accept Christ's command to take the gospel to all the gentile nations of the world. The thought was too radical for them to comprehend. Finally, it took a miraculous vision of unclean animals, a message from an angel, and two men knocking on the door of Simon the tanner in Joppa before the Jewish apostle Peter would enter the house of Cornelius the Gentile.

Even after Cornelius and his household came to Christ and were baptized in the Holy Spirit and in water, the Jewish believing leaders in Jerusalem were not happy: "Now the apostles and brethren who were in Judea heard that the Gentiles had also received the word of God. And when Peter came up to Jerusalem, those of the circumcision contended with him, saying, 'You went in to uncircumcised men and ate with them!'" (Acts 11:1–3).

It does not seem that these Jewish followers of Jesus were all too excited about Peter's gentile adventure! What were the neighbors going to think! After Peter explained what had occurred, the Jewish leaders were awestruck—even shocked that Gentiles could come into a salvation that was historically Jewish in nature: "And as I began to speak, the Holy Spirit fell upon them, as upon us at the beginning. Then I remembered the word of the Lord, how he said, 'John indeed baptized with water, but you shall be baptized with the Holy Spirit.' If therefore God gave them the same gift as He gave us when we believed on the Lord Jesus Christ, who was I that I could withstand God? When they heard these things they became silent; and they glorified God, saying, 'Then God has also granted to the Gentiles repentance to life'" (Acts 11:15–18).

Thank God! You can only imagine the religious and cultural lines that had to be crossed in order to open wide the doors to the entire gentile world. This was the faith of the Jews. For centuries, it was the Jews who preserved the promises and the covenants and now these Jewish leaders who had received Jesus recognized that the Gentiles had also been granted repentance unto life. Their immediate response to God was "whosoever will!" This is why Paul, the Pharisee of Pharisees, the Hebrew of Hebrews, was so forceful in his letter to the Ephesians. Listen again to his lesson about the Hebraic roots of these Ephesian believers:

That at that time you were without Christ, being aliens from the commonwealth of Israel and strangers from the covenants of promise, having no hope and without God in the world. But now in Christ Jesus you who once were far off have been brought near by the blood of Christ. For He Himself is our peace, who has made both one, and has broken down the middle wall of separation, having abolished in His flesh the enmity, that is, the law of commandments contained in ordinances, so as to create in Himself one new man from the two, thus making peace, and that He might reconcile them both to God in one body through the cross, thereby putting to death the enmity. And He came and preached peace to you who were afar off [Gentiles] and to those who were near [Jews]. For through Him we both have access by one Spirit to the Father. Now, therefore, you are no longer strangers and foreigners, but fellow citizens with the saints and members of the household of God, having been built on the foundation of the apostles and prophets, Jesus Christ Himself being the chief cornerstone (Eph. 2:12–20).

Great News for Gentiles!

Paul is in effect saying: "Do you have any idea who you are in Jesus—the Jewish Messiah? You have been called uncircumcised

Gentiles by circumcised Jews for centuries. You were pagans, living outside of any hope or promise! But now you have been brought into the faith that my fathers and I have nurtured and preserved all of these years. You're not traveling down some other parallel pathway, but you are part of the same covenant roots that we Jews enjoy! You are not 'foreigners' who do not have the rights of citizenship but you are now part of the 'commonwealth of Israel' and have full rights! You are 'fellow citizens with the saints.'" The saints that Paul speaks about in verse 19 are the saints of old. He is saying that Gentiles have become part of the root system that stretches all the way back to Abraham, Isaac, and Jacob. They are also members of the same Jewish household, able to enjoy all of the covenantal blessings that God gave to Abraham. On top of it all, these Gentiles are coming into a house that has a firm foundation of Jewish apostles, Jewish prophets and a Jewish Messiah—Jesus. Look at Paul's usage of the word "one" in the book of Ephesians: "For He Himself is our peace, who has made both ONE [Jew and gentile believers], and has broken down the middle wall of separation, having abolished in His flesh the enmity, that is, the law of commandments contained in ordinances, so as to create in Himself ONE new man from the two [Jewish and gentile believers], thus making peace, and that He might reconcile them both to God in ONE body through the cross, thereby putting to death the enmity" (Eph. 2:14–16).

In the temple courts there stood a middle wall separating the court of the Jews from the court of the Gentile. Paul tells the Ephesian Christians that through Jesus this middle wall of separation has been broken down and now both Jews and Gentiles can worship together as one! Under the old covenant any Gentile who desired to worship the living God was welcome, but never lost their standing as "strangers" or "foreigners." Paul is proclaiming to these gentile believers that they have a new standing with Jewish believers: ONE new man! No longer strangers and foreigners! All the walls of division and separation have been broken down!

You can only imagine that hearing such things from a Jew of Paul's stature, heritage, and scholarly reputation, brought great freedom to the Ephesians. Paul further clarifies how far God was willing to go in breaking down the walls separating Gentiles from the promises: "There is ONE body and ONE Spirit, just as you were called in ONE hope of your calling; ONE Lord, ONE faith, ONE baptism; ONE God and Father of all, who is above all, and through all, and in you all" (Eph. 4:4–6).

One Covenant Not Two

Yes, in Jesus, Jews and Gentiles become one but this in no way nullifies God's specific plan, purpose, and covenant with the nation of Israel as a whole. This being said, for the apostle Paul there were not two covenants—one for Jew and one for Gentile. There were not two faiths—one for Jew and one for Gentile. There were not two baptisms or two Messiahs—one for Jew and the other for Gentile. Paul goes to great lengths to persuade the Ephesian believers that the cross is the passageway that brings them into the same spiritual inheritance as the Jews: "...and that He might reconcile them both to God in one body through the cross, thereby putting to death the enmity" (Eph. 2:16). In his letter to the Galatians Paul makes the point again: "Christ has redeemed us from the curse of the law, having become a curse for us (for it is written, 'cursed is everyone who hangs on a tree'), that the blessing of Abraham might come upon the Gentiles in Christ Jesus...." (Gal. 3:13–14).

Knowing the depths to which God has gone to rescue Gentiles from the nations and bring them into the nourishing sap of the olive tree, how can we ever conclude the Christian faith can be truly authentic aside from the spiritual commonwealth of Israel? Has the modern church grasped the significance of the fact that we serve the God of Israel—the God of Abraham, Isaac, and Jacob—the God of the Jews?

No Identity Outside of Israel

The church has no identity outside of her relationship with Israel. God has chosen to reveal Himself as the God of Israel. If you want to discover anything about God, past, present, or future, you can only know Him in connection to Israel. If you disconnect God from Israel you no longer have the God of the Bible. You have a god that you have designed, but he is not the God of Abraham. A Christianity that is not connected to the restoration of the Jews to their Messiah has lost the dynamic of the apostolic faith. God is a God of history and the specific history in which He can be found is the history of Israel and only Israel. The way that He deals with Israel in judgment and mercy, exile and restoration, severity and blessing, is God's way of revealing His character to the world. First Corinthians 10:11 explains how God related to the people of Israel so as to make His historical relationship with them a teaching tool for us: "Now all these things happened to them as examples, and they were written for our admonition, upon whom the ends of the ages have come."

Speaking of the relationship between God and Israel, the late Arthur Katz has this to say:

This may well account for the woefully inadequate knowledge of God so rampant in the modern church. We have not understood the severity of God toward Israel in judgments that have fallen upon that nation, nor in that which will yet befall them. If He did not spare Israel, and indeed, has temporarily cut them off from the root of God, then will He spare us if we do not abide in faith? The absence of fear toward God and the knowledge of His judgments are altogether, in our opinion, directly related to the absence of our knowledge of God's direct dealing with Israel in judgment. Our witness, therefore, to Israel is equally as inadequate. Something is lacking that would have brought us to a texture of the faith, to an integrity of the faith, and to a sense of identification of things future that could only be ours because of God's past relationship with Israel and what He prophetically declares of Israel's future.[1]

137

By distancing ourselves from our connection to Israel we have also distanced ourselves from the God who has chosen Israel as His representative. If a Christian does not see himself as a part of the history of the Jews he does not carry with him the depth of meaning, wonder, and understanding a person of history shepherds. A Christian's history is often only retraced to the time of his salvation. Because he does not see himself as a sojourner of faith—in a long line of sojourners from ages past—the blessed hope of the Lord's return has been dimmed. If we do not know where we came from, how will we know where we are going?

Because Christianity has forgotten that its history is rooted in Israel's history, it is given over to a new cultural Christianity. We move quickly from one fad to the next, and from one social issue to the next, because we have forgotten that our story has much deeper roots than what might be popular or faddish today.

Why was this Jewish man Paul so adamant about communicating the Jewish origin of the Ephesian Gentiles' faith? Remember, this is the same Paul who said of himself: "Circumcised the eighth day, of the stock of Israel, of the tribe of Benjamin, a Hebrew of the Hebrews; concerning the law, a Pharisee; concerning zeal, persecuting the church; concerning the righteousness which is in the law, blameless" (Phil. 3:5–6).

Why is Paul willing to be accursed in order that his Jewish countrymen might come to faith? Why would a man who met the Lord on the Damascus Road, who was caught up to the third heaven and tasted the glories of the eternal realm, be willing to trade all of that so that Jewish people might believe? Notice the extent that Paul is willing to go for this to happen: "I tell you the truth I am not lying, my conscience also bearing me witness in the Holy Spirit, that I have great sorrow and continual grief in my heart. For I could wish that I myself were accursed from Christ for my brethren, my countrymen according to the flesh, who are Israelites, to whom pertain the adoption, the glory, the covenants, the giving of the law, the service of God, and the promises; of whom are the fathers and from whom, according to the flesh, Christ came…." (Rom. 9:1–5).

The Mystery of the Gospel

Why does Paul place so much importance on the reconciliation of Jew and gentile believers in Messiah? The answer is that Paul understood the mystery of God. The things Paul wrote concerning this mystery are still (for the most part) a mystery today. The mystery of the gospel which was so central to Paul's teaching is still hidden from the understanding of many. Our prophetic destiny will come into fullness when we understand this mystery.

Understanding the mysteries of God requires soberness and reverence. There are certain things that are so tender to the heart of God that He only unveils them to those who are loyal to the revelation behind them. When God first revealed to the early church what He had hidden for ages, they loyally set out to communicate what was in God's heart—unashamedly and passionately.

However, as we have seen in this book, as the gospel spread to the gentile world, Christian leaders were smitten with jealousy toward the Jews and arrogantly began to boast against them. Paul, prophetically foreseeing this would happen, warned the gentile believers:

And if some of the branches were broken off, and you, being a wild olive tree, were grafted in among them, and with them became a partaker of the root and fatness of the olive tree, do not boast against the branches. But if you do boast, remember that you do not support the root, but the root supports you. You will say then, "Branches were broken off that I might be grafted in." Well said. Because of unbelief they were broken off, and you stand by faith. Do not be haughty, but fear. For if God did not spare the natural branches, He may not spare you either. Therefore consider the goodness and severity of God: on those who fell, severity, but toward you, goodness, if you continue in His goodness. Otherwise you also will be cut off (Rom. 11:17–22).

Has the church been cut off from our nourishing roots because of centuries of boasting against Jewish branches? It's something to think about, isn't it? Have we developed the haughty spirit Paul warned us about? Proverbs 16:18 says: "Pride goes before destruction, and a haughty spirit before a fall." When you begin to understand the mystery Paul is speaking of, it's as if a door opens into a large furnished room you have never been in before. Suddenly, your faith is connected to a past that is connected with the God of Israel's history. You are part of a divine plan conceived in God's heart before the world began.

Just what is the mystery of the gospel? The reason it is so vague is because the subject is avoided in most pulpits. It would not be uncommon for a person to spend a lifetime listening to the teaching of God's Word and never hear a message on this mystery. The divide between Christians and Jews runs deep. To avoid this subject is to avoid the greatest statement of faith concerning God's eternal purpose, divine wisdom, and unsearchable character. To avoid this mystery is to miss the significance of the high priestly prayer of Jesus in John 17:20–23. The mystery is found in several passages of Scripture. Let's first take a look in Romans: "Oh, the depth of the riches both of the wisdom and knowledge of God! How unsearchable are His judgments and His ways past finding out! For who has known the mind of the Lord? Or who has become His counselor? Or who has first given to Him and it shall be repaid to Him? For of Him and through Him and to Him are all things, to whom be glory forever, Amen" (Rom. 11:33–36).

What has Paul seen that we have not yet seen? What is he so overjoyed about? When Paul opens his discourse on the mystery of God in Romans 9, he says that through the Jewish people came the covenants and the promises. But of course, this historical people rejected their Messiah and have been partially blinded by their unbelief. Paul asks whether somehow this makes God unrighteous because He has presently hardened them:

What shall we say then? Is there unrighteousness with God? Certainly not! For He says to Moses, "I will have mercy on whomever I will have mercy, and I will have compassion on whomever I will have compassion." So then it is not of him who wills, nor of him who runs, but of God who shows mercy. For the Scripture says to the Pharaoh, "For this very purpose I have raised you up, that I may show My power in you, and that My name may be declared in all the earth." Therefore He has mercy on whom He wills, and whom He wills He hardens (Rom. 9:14–18).

Paul is overwhelmed that God in His mercy allowed His chosen people to be broken off for a season in order to make a way for the Gentiles to come to faith: "I say then, have they [the Jews] stumbled that they should fall? Certainly not! But through their fall, to provoke them to jealousy, salvation has come to the Gentiles" (Rom. 11:11).

Paul sees the divine mystery: The Jews fell away in order that salvation might come to the Gentiles! In this same verse, Paul clearly sees that the restoration of the natural branches (Israel) are dependent on the unnatural branches (the gentile believers). The present role of gentile Christians is to provoke the Jews to jealousy. This little word "provoke" means to "come alongside someone and to cause him to boil or seethe with jealousy." Presently, the believing Gentile who is now part of the same root system as the Jew, is to come alongside Jewish people that have not received Jesus and minister to them (we will find out how to do this in chapters 9 and 10). Where did Paul come up with the divine mystery that Gentiles needed Jews in order to come into the faith, and Jews need Gentiles in order to be grafted back in again? Where did he get the idea that part of the divine mystery would be gentile Christians lovingly coming alongside of Jews who have not received Yeshua (Jesus) to provoke them to jealousy in order that they might be saved? The mystery is clearly unveiled by Moses centuries earlier when he records God's words concerning His future dealings with the Jewish people: "They have provoked Me to jealousy by what is not God; they have moved Me to anger by their foolish idols. But I will provoke them to jealousy by those who are not a nation; I will move them to anger by a foolish nation" (Deut. 32:21).

Paul tells us that when the Jewish nation is provoked to jealousy by gentile believers whom God has drawn from the nations of the world, a great measure of rich blessing will flow to the entire world: "Now if their fall is riches for the world, and their failure riches for the Gentiles, how much more their fullness!" (Rom. 11:12). "For if their being cast away is the reconciling of the world, what will their acceptance be but life from the dead?" (Rom. 11:15).

Presently, a partial blindness has come to Israel: "For I do not desire, brethren, that you should be ignorant of this mystery, lest you should be wise in your own opinion, that blindness in part has happened to Israel until the fullness of the Gentiles has come in" (Rom. 11:25).

Drawing Out a People for His Name

God is presently drawing out a righteous remnant of gentile believers from the nations of the world. Our missionary efforts in evangelizing the nations are directly linked to Israel's restoration! "Simon has declared how God at the first visited the Gentiles to take out of them a people for His name" (Acts 15:14).

Here is the most critical question for the American church today: How can Christians make Israel jealous unto salvation if we have not first been reconciled to her? Jesus is waiting for us—the gentile believing community of faith—to restore this long divided relationship and come alongside Jewish people the world over. Until we do, the King's final consummation of all things will not begin. The apostle Peter understood the critical need for restoration when he proclaimed in his first sermon: "...and that He may send Jesus Christ, who was preached to you before, whom heaven must receive until the times of restoration of all things, which God has spoken by the mouth of all His holy prophets since the world began" (Acts 3:20–21).

Here are four aspects of the mystery of the gospel from what we have seen so far:

1. Because Jews fell away, a door was opened so that Gentiles might come to faith in the Jewish Messiah.

2. The present role of believing Gentiles is to make Jews jealous to the point that they come to faith in Jesus their Messiah. Gentiles needed them in order to come into the faith, and Jews need Gentiles in order to return.

3. Gentiles who are being saved from the nations hold the key to Israel's restoration.

4. There is a fourth part to this mystery, and it's the part that brought Paul so much clarity and expressive joy: "For if their being cast away is the reconciling of the world, what will their acceptance be but life from the dead?" (Rom. 11:15).

When Jewish people who have been broken off are restored it will cause a great revival in the earth. When the gentile church embraces this mystery and reconciles itself with God's eternal purpose, which He has chosen to accomplish through the restoration of the relationship between Jewish and gentile believers—then and only then will the world be anxious to hear the message of the gospel! Now you know why Paul—the once proud Hebrew of Hebrews— was so intense in communicating to Gentiles the importance of their Jewish heritage. If they would somehow miss the importance of understanding the glorious meaning of the divine mystery of the gospel, the final harvest would not be consummated. That's why Paul was willing to be shipwrecked, imprisoned, and eventually martyred for the sake of this mystery. Paul, the Jew, spent his life as the apostle to the Gentiles. He knew they were the key to his countrymen's salvation. Listen, as Paul explains the mystery to the Ephesian gentile believers:

For this reason I, Paul, the prisoner of Christ Jesus for you Gentiles—if indeed you have heard of the dispensation of the grace of God which was given to me for you, how that by revelation He made known to me the MYSTERY (as I have briefly written already, by which, when you read, you may understand my knowledge in the MYSTERY of Christ), which in other ages was not made known to the sons of men, as it has now been revealed by the Spirit to His holy apostles and prophets:

That the Gentiles should be fellow heirs, of the same body, and partakers of His promise in Christ through the gospel, of which I became a minister according to the gift of the grace of God given to me by the effective working of His power. To me, who am less than the least of all the saints, this grace was given, that I should preach among the Gentiles the unsearchable riches of Christ, and to make all see what is the fellowship of the MYSTERY, which from the beginning of the ages has been hidden in God who created all things through Jesus Christ; to the intent that now the manifold wisdom of God might be made known by the church to the principalities and powers in the heavenly places (Eph. 3:1–10).

Did you catch the mystery? It's in verse 6: "that the Gentiles should be fellow heirs, of the same body, and partakers of His promise in Christ through the gospel." It's also in verse 9 where Paul speaks of "the fellowship of the mystery." This is the rich fellowship between righteous gentile believers who have come alongside righteous Jewish believers. Together as one new man these saints proclaim the "manifold wisdom of God" (v. 10) to the powers in the heavenly realms. And what message does the fellowship of Jewish and gentile believers send to the demonic principalities and powers? The message is clear: In the infinite wisdom of God He allowed His own covenant people to be broken off for a season—that He might draw a people (who were not a people of a commonwealth that included eternal covenants and blessings) to Himself from the nations of the world. And, those would be the very people—though historically at enmity with His chosen people—who would commit themselves to the chosen's salvation. In God's wisdom, when those two people with historical hatred and enmity are reconciled to each other, it is the key that unlocks the reconciliation of all things to Himself. Glory to God in the highest!

This reconciliation of Jew and Gentile in Jesus for the ultimate salvation of the world is the mystery of the gospel! The very heart of this mystery is found in the high priestly prayer of Jesus which we saw earlier:

I do not pray for these [Jews] alone, but also for those [Gentiles] who will believe in Me through their [Jews] word; that they all [Jews and Gentiles in Messiah] may be one, as You, Father, are in Me, and I in You; that they [Jews and Gentiles] may be one in Us, that the world may believe that You sent Me. And the glory which You gave Me I have given them [Jews and Gentiles together], that they may be one just as We are one; I in them [Jews and Gentiles], and You in Me; that they may be made perfect in one, and that the world may know that You have sent Me, and have loved them as You have loved Me (John 17:20–23).

What restoration could have greater odds? As we have seen so far, what two people over the centuries of time have had more enmity and animosity than Christians and Jews? For 1,900 years Satan has succeeded in driving us apart. The idea that the church has replaced Israel comes from the belief that God is finished with Israel. If this is our conclusion it will lead us to the arrogant belief that the church itself is the Kingdom and through her alone will God consummate all things.

A church that triumphantly boasts against the Jews is doing so in opposition to the God of the Jews. This demeans God's choice and questions His infinite wisdom. When Paul grasped the depth of the mystery of the gospel he was at a loss for words. All he could say was: "Oh, the depth of the riches both of the wisdom and knowledge of God! How unsearchable are His judgments and His ways past finding out!" (Rom. 11:33).

That God would choose this pathway to reconcile the world to Himself is a distasteful prospect to many churchmen, and so they refuse to embrace it. They refuse because they despise God's choice of Israel to begin with. This is why for centuries they have done everything to remove Israel from any connection to God's covenants and promises. This is why they have avoided the mystery of the gospel. The mystery in itself promises Israel's restoration—a restoration that many churchmen cannot fathom or accept. However, the fulfillment of this mystery after so many years of being hidden under the cloak of Replacement Theology and jealousy is today the greatest issue of the church. Will we choose the easy, less authentic path or something of heavenly order and eternal value? Remember, true loyalty to God is to hear and obey His Word in the power of the Holy Spirit.

The Coming Revolution of Restoration

This book serves as a two minute warning. Time is short. The hour is late and the bridegroom is soon to appear. Before He comes He is sending to His church a revolution of restoration! His high priestly prayer at the Last Supper will be fulfilled. Jew and Gentile will be restored in Messiah. This new relationship in itself will become a proclamation to the principalities and powers in the heavenly realms: "Muster the angelic armies! The restoration of all things has begun! Earth's final consummation is soon! The enmity between Jew and Gentile has been forever broken by the power of the cross! We are one in Jesus—Yeshua, our Jewish Messiah! Together we are the commonwealth of Israel! We are people of the Book! We are people of history and we serve the God of history—the God of the Jews, from whom came salvation! We are now being built together on the Hebraic roots of Jewish apostles and prophets—Jesus being the Chief Cornerstone! This is the infinite wisdom of God." This restored relationship will rally the angelic hosts to attention as they prepare for the coming of the Lord and the final harvest of souls.

The relationship between Jew and Gentile in Messiah will cause fear and dread to run through the ranks of demonic principalities and powers in the heavenly realms. They have cunningly severed this union for centuries. They fear the exponential power that will be expressed through the "one new man"—the restored fellowship of Jew and Gentile in Messiah. The wisdom of God is proclaimed in this living word picture. The awesome power of God to reconcile two people together under His banner will be a signal to the adversary of our souls that the world itself will soon be reconciled to the Lord of Glory. It is now the hour that we turn our attention to the roots of our faith and commit ourselves to rallying around the righteous remnant of Jewish believers the world over. Jesus is depending on us to be ministers of reconciliation. The identity of who the church is will never be fully authentic until we restore our fellowship with our elder brothers—the Jews. The world can never be reconciled to God until we rally around the believing Jewish remnant (of which there are now several hundred thousand) and, together as the "one new man" in Messiah, provoke the Jewish people who have not met Messiah, to jealousy. This restoration is the key that unlocks the final harvest of the earth and the final reconciliation of all things to God through Christ. In our next chapter we will show you how this restoration can be fulfilled.

The Olive Tree

Once the chosen mission of Israel is denied,
the entire foundation of Christianity is taken away.
Roy Eckardt

God elected a certain nation to be His bondslave,
and through that nation a knowledge of His
salvation is to come to all the world.
Oswald Chambers

The Mount of Olives in Jerusalem acquired its name because of the olive trees that grow on its slopes. The Garden of Gethsemane where Jesus often prayed with His disciples is located at the base of the mountain. Gethsemane ("Gat Shemanim" in Hebrew) means olive press. There are olive trees in the garden that date back before the time of Christ. And yes, they are still fruitful.

The olive tree is virtually indestructible. You can cut it down, but little shoots will soon blossom from the severed trunk, and a new tree will form. However, a tree that grows from seed or shoot will produce a poor yield. In order to produce the maximum yield, shoots from cultivated trees are grafted into other cultivated trees. In the Scripture, olive oil is spoken of often. It was used for medicine and lighting lamps. It was also used to anoint prophets, priests, and kings. The olive leaf in the mouth of a dove was the first sign that the waters had begun to recede during the great Flood.

The Spiritual Commonwealth of Israel

Olive trees are not majestic. Their branches are gnarly and aged. To look at an olive tree makes you wonder how anything so old looking could produce anything. Paul the apostle uses the metaphor of the aged, cultivated olive tree to describe the spiritual common- wealth of Israel. The natural branches are the people of Israel while the wild olive shoots that are engrafted into the spiritual common- wealth of God are Gentiles who have come to faith. Paul says that this grafting of wild olive shoots into a cultivated tree is contrary to nature. Normally, it is a cultivated olive branch that is grafted into a cultivated tree. Wild olive trees are unproductive until they are cul- tivated. Thus, gentile wild shoots are only productive because God by his mercy has grafted them in with Israel—the cultivated shoots. Paul says this should remove all boasting from gentile Christians:

And if some of the branches were broken off, and you, being a wild olive tree were grafted in among them, and with them became a partaker of the root and fatness of the olive tree, do not boast against the branches. But if you do boast, remember that you do not support the root, but the root supports you. You will say then, "Branches were broken off that I might be grafted in." Well said. Because of unbelief they were broken off, and you stand by faith. Do not be haughty, but fear. For if God did not spare the natural branches, He may not spare you either. Therefore consider the goodness and severity of God: on those who fell, severity; but toward you, goodness, if you continue in His goodness. Otherwise you also will be cut off. And they also if they do not continue in unbe- lief, will be grafted in, for God is able to graft them in again. For if you were cut out of the olive tree which is wild by nature, and were grafted contrary to nature into a cultivated olive tree, how much more will these, who are natural branches, be grafted into their own olive tree? (Rom. 11:17–24).

Something of supernatural importance is happening in the earth in our day! Jesus, our Jewish Messiah is gathering a righteous remnant of gentile and Jewish believers. Right now there is a great awakening within the worldwide Jewish community. Thousands of Jews the world over are coming to faith in Jesus. The number of Jewish believers now stands conservatively at two hundred and fifty thousand—an unprecedented number. Nothing like this has ever happened before. The opening of their blind eyes to Messiah is a wonderful sign of the Lord's soon appearance. Jews are now being grafted back into the olive tree—the spiritual commonwealth of Israel! Engrafted within this cultivated olive tree is a righteous remnant of gentile believers who see themselves as a part of Israel rather than separate from Israel. This remnant has always existed but a new awakening by the Holy Spirit is exponentially increasing its influence. Grafting wild olive shoots into the natural branches of a cultivated olive tree (even though contrary to nature) will bring supernatural rapid growth. When Jews (the natural branches) and Gentiles (wild branches) who have been grafted into the deep rooted olive tree of Israel and become one in Messiah, you can expect God's manifest glory to be expressed. The fruit of this union of Jew and Gentile will be pressed together like olives in the presses of "Gat Shemanim"—Gethsemane. As the oil of God's anointing flows from these two people being "pressed" together as one, the yokes of bondage Satan has used to prevent a worldwide harvest will be broken. In speaking of Israel's future restoration, the prophet Isaiah speaks of a great anointing that will come upon Jews and Gentiles who together seek the Messiah:

The remnant will return, the remnant of Jacob, to the Mighty God. For though your people, O Israel, be as the sand of the sea, a remnant of them will return; the destruction decreed shall overflow with righteousness....It shall come to pass in that day that his burden will be taken

*away from your shoulder, and his yoke from your neck, AND THE
YOKE WILL BE DESTROYED BECAUSE OF THE ANOINT-
ING OIL....And in that day there shall be a Root of Jesse, who shall
stand as a banner to the people; for the Gentiles shall seek Him, and His
resting place shall be glorious* (Isa. 10:21–22, 27; 11:10).

Satan's Worst Nightmare

Beloved, we are in a critical time in the American church. Presently, forty to fifty percent of American Christians embrace Replacement Theology—the idea that Israel no longer plays a role in God's
covenant. We have seen in the last two chapters that because of our
severed roots with Israel our families and our churches are in serious
condition. If we do not embrace what the Lord is doing in this hour
and restore our biblical and Hebraic heritage, the hemorrhage will
continue. This is the warning this book is heralding.

There is something else that stands at a critical juncture as well:
The future world harvest of souls. Jesus is preparing for the final harvest of the earth and He desires for you to embrace the revolution of
restoration. The church, as we know it is now being separated from
the Lord as a shepherd separates the sheep from the goats, based
upon its love and concern for the brethren of Jesus—the Jewish
people. However, a righteous remnant of Gentiles will be supernaturally knit together with the believing Jewish remnant. Interlocked
into the same root, these Jewish and gentile believers in Jesus will
become one, just as Jesus prayed in John 17. They will become the
"one new man" Paul spoke about in Ephesians 2. The world has
never seen the full impact this restoration will have upon planet
earth. This restoration is Satan's worst nightmare. For centuries, Satan has succeeded in severing the roots that bind us together, thus
destroying our exponential power. Incredibly, Satan has used the
gentile engrafted branches to cut off the Jewish natural branches.
The adversary will use every diabolical tool at his disposal to keep
Jewish and gentile believers in Jesus severed at the root. The alter-

native is unacceptable to the enemy of our souls. When we are fully restored (and we will be—you can be sure of it) the final harvest of souls will be reaped with the sharp sickle of the Lord Himself, and Satan's kingdom will crumble in ruins.

We said in our last chapter that the issue of Israel is at the center of God's eternal purpose of reconciling all things to Himself. That God would choose to make the restoration of Israel the key to the world's reconciliation is in fact His eternal mystery. And yet, as we have seen, gentile Christians play a key role in this reconciliation. The decision made by gentile believers to come alongside the Jewish people and make them jealous unto salvation is a strategic end-time mandate from the Lord of eternity. What could be more foolish and despised as this? There are no two people that have been at more historical odds than Jews and confessing Christians. If Christians find it difficult walking in unity with one another, how can they reconcile with Jews? And yet, ultimately our own identification and transformation into Christ's likeness will not be complete until we come near to His brethren—the Jewish people. After 1,900 years of persecuting our elder brothers, it can only be a work of the Holy Spirit that will draw them to a jealousy of a holy kind.

Capturing the Heart of God

The mandate of our mission of restoration is not simply developing a new outlook about Jews. God is asking more of us than just changing our minds. He is asking us to change our hearts. He desires that we have the same passion for Israel as His Son. As Jesus approached Jerusalem He wept over a people who were like sheep without a shepherd. If our hearts break over the lost sheep of the House of Israel then we have captured God's heart. God desires for us to have a passion for the nation of Israel as Paul did.

We saw in our last chapter the extent to which the apostle Paul was willing to go in order that Jewish people might come to faith in Yeshua (Jesus). Let's investigate this further. Was Paul willing to give up his eternal destiny for the Jews because of his own ethnic identity with them? Was this simply a Jewish man having some kind of natural affinity for his own flesh and blood? Actually, Paul's passion to minister to the Jews had more to do with his fellowship with Christ than with the fact that he was Jewish: "I tell you the truth in Christ; I am not lying, my conscience also bearing me witness in the Holy Spirit, that I have great sorrow and continual grief in my heart. For I could wish that I myself were accursed from Christ for my brethren, my countrymen according to the flesh" (Rom. 9:1–3).

Paul's love for the Jew was greatly motivated by his union with Christ in the Holy Spirit: "I tell the truth in Christ...in the Holy Spirit." This love flowed first from Paul's spiritual man. Yes, the Jewish people were Paul's "brethren according to the flesh," but his loving compassion for them came from a deeper well than his own heart. It flowed from the heart of the Messiah for the Jewish people. This is our starting point as well. If gentile Christians, out of a love for Jesus, are willing to love Jewish people who have not yet found Messiah, the process of restoration will one day be fulfilled. No, it will not be easy, for nothing of this historical magnitude could be. There is too much at risk for the powers of darkness to let down their guard on this ongoing enmity. There is too much water under the proverbial bridge—too many scars and wounds on both sides—and Satan will want to keep it that way.

The world still awaits this historical divide to be healed. Yes, gentile Christians have come into the nourishing root of the olive tree in order to share their faith with Jewish people, but how can we ever make them jealous of our relationship with Yeshua if we do not carry Yeshua's love for them in our hearts? It was Messiah's love that drew Saul—later Paul. It was Messiah's love that drew Nicodemus. Here were two Hebrew scholars that without a supernatural manifestation of love would have never been drawn to the Messiah.

The issue of the people of Israel who have not come to faith in Jesus has been a stumbling stone for many Gentiles over the centuries. As we have seen, a triumphal arrogance has persisted in Christians toward Jews who reject Jesus. It continues festering like an open wound even today. Today, modern Israel is a nation that seemingly misunderstands its own calling and destiny in God. Even though they have been chosen as God's standard bearers, there seems to be a rejection of that divine choice. For the most part, Israel as a nation is given over to secular humanism and atheism. Vice, corruption, and prostitution are growing problems. Abortion, alcoholism, and drug addiction are all on the rise within Israel's borders. Israel has become a nation not unlike the other nations of the world. She has in many ways rejected her prophetic destiny. As well, there is a growing persecution against Messianic believers by certain elements within the orthodox community. Several Messianic congregational meeting places have been fire bombed.

A Love That Requires the Transformation of the Holy Spirit

In the natural, becoming ministers of reconciliation to the Jewish community inside and outside of Israel seems hopeless. Why bother? The answer lies in why Paul the apostle bothered. Paul knew that a gentile church that was loyal to God's eternal purpose of reconciling Jew and Gentile together as one new man, was the key to fulfilling the seventy-three words of the prayer of Jesus in John chapter 17. What is at stake here is the glory of God being expressed through that reconciled relationship—thus opening the passageway for the final harvest. And, astonishingly, in the infinite wisdom of God, He has determined the success of this seemingly impossible reconciliation to be initiated by a gentile church which has no natural affinity for Jews.

This is why our love for Jewish people cannot be natural. We must have what Paul had—a love born completely out of relationship with Christ through the power of the Holy Spirit. To embrace such a spiritual love will require the gentile church to experience a transformation that only comes through the work of the Holy Spirit. Only when this happens will gentile Christians ever come into their prophetic destiny. The very expression of this sacrificial love proclaims the infinite wisdom of God. For God to allow His chosen people to be broken off so that He could draw in a people from the nations of the world is in fact, His infinite wisdom and eternal mystery. He has called these believing Gentiles to walk with such authentic love for His chosen that when Jews who have not met Yeshua look into their faces they see the love of Messiah and are made jealous unto salvation. For a secular, humanistic Jew, there is nothing more powerfully authentic and real than this.

If this sounds unreasonable and unnatural it's because it is. God's mysteries and infinite wisdom are never compatible with the natural man. That is why they are only born of the Spirit within the spiritual man. Our mandate is to fulfill the prayer of Jesus in John 17—that Jewish and gentile believers would become one. Keep in mind that when Jesus prayed this prayer there were only Jewish believers. As we have seen, Jewish believers in the early church needed to cross major cultural boundaries in order to proclaim the gospel to Gentiles. Today, there are hundreds of millions of gentile Christians and only a few hundred thousand Jewish believers. After 1,900 years of Christian persecution of Jews, it is no wonder why Jewish people are afraid of our faith. We must begin now to develop the kind of oneness in relationship with our believing Jewish brothers and sisters that Jesus prayed about. Again, this relationship with the Messianic believing community is the key to God's glory being expressed through the church (made up of both Jewish and gentile believers) to the world.

And yet, if our love is exclusively for those Jews who believe in Jesus, we completely miss the heart of God. As the Lord continues to restore Jewish and gentile believers together as one new man, a caution is necessary: this re-born unity of believers is never to the exclusion of love for Jews who have not come to faith in Jesus the

Messiah. Gentile Christians have a responsibility to carry such an authentic love for Jewish people who are not yet in the Way, that it brings them to jealousy and ultimately, salvation. When they see this supernatural love they will know that it is of a quality so deep and rich that only their God—the God Abraham, Isaac, and Jacob could have placed it in the heart of a Gentile who in the natural sense is at odds with them.

For a Christian to love a Jew only because they have come to faith in Jesus is not a spiritual love at all. It's a natural love inspired by the same Triumphalism and Supercessionism that has been sewn into the gentile church for centuries. This kind of natural love basically says to the Jew: "We will love you when you come over to our side. We will accept you when you think like we think and believe what we believe. Only when you convert to our way will we love you." This kind of natural affinity is born out of historic Christian gentile pride and arrogance toward Jews. As well, it dishonors God's divine choice and His eternal covenant with the Jews. Yes, most Jews have rejected Messiah, but in God's mercy He will one day restore them. Out of obedience to His divine choice we must love and honor them as God does.

It would be like a legalistic Christian saying to a sinner: "When you dress like we dress, act like we act, and attend our church regularly, then we will accept you. Until then, we want nothing to do with you because you are a sinner." This is why legalistic churches are so small and exclusive—sinners see their condescending, arrogant, conditional love and are repelled by it. There are between fifteen and eighteen million Jewish people in the world who are desperately in need of a Savior's love. Will we love them in spite of the fact they presently reject Jesus? Will we weep over them as Jesus wept? Will we ask the Holy Spirit to fill our hearts with a supernatural love for them as Paul had?

When we catch the eternal purpose of God in reconciling the nation that bears His holy name, first to Himself and then to us, the world will finally experience the manifestation of God's glory Jesus prayed for in those seventy-three epic words in John 17. May we ask Father God to fill our hearts with the same kind of love that was in the apostle Paul—a love that had more to do with a supernatural work of the Spirit within his heart than with his own Jewishness. In speaking of reaching out to Jews who have not met Yeshua, Paul declares: "How then shall they call on Him in whom they have not believed? And how shall they believe in Him of whom they have not heard? And how shall they hear without a preacher? And how shall they preach unless they are sent? As it is written: How beautiful are the feet of those who preach the gospel of peace, who bring glad tidings of good things!" (Rom. 10:14–15).

After 1,900 years of trampling under foot the Jews who do not believe in Jesus—often times ostracizing them from the gentile Christian community into locked ghettos until they agreed to convert or worse yet giving them the choice of baptism or death, it is high time we set aside our arrogance and unconditionally love Jewish people—whether or not they convert to our faith. This, for the most part, is our attitude towards the rest of the unbelieving world—why should it be any different with Jews who are not yet followers of the Way. We give to the poor of the world regardless of their beliefs, so why would it be any different with poor Jews—regardless of their beliefs?

The gospel of shalom (peace) is filled with glad tidings and good things—not with a triumphal pride and arrogance which says: "We have the truth, and you don't; we follow in the Way, and you have rejected it." Our feet were never meant to trample Jewish people. Instead, for those who choose to share Yeshua's love with Jews, He gives to them beautiful feet as they proclaim Shalom.

It is time for the restoration to begin. From our depth of love and loyalty to Jesus there are certain things Christians need to let go. There are issues at the core of the division between Jews and Gentiles that need to be addressed. We believe that once these issues are healed, our own identity in Christ will be restored, and the restoration with our elder brothers, especially those within the household of faith, will begin.

Chosenness

The issue that has caused the deepest hurt and jealousy in gentile Christians toward Jews is the little word "chosen." The early gentile church was so offended by the Jewish claim to being God's chosen people, they claimed it for themselves. The gentile Christians believed Jews were forever rejected because of their blindness towards Jesus. The church taught that they themselves were now the new "Israel of God"—the new "chosen people." Islam has also seethed with jealousy towards the Jews being the chosen. They solved the problem by simply declaring Abraham to be a Muslim— case closed.

The Jews are hated even to this day because of the jealousy over who is chosen. In fact, the Jewish continual claim to chosenness is very possibly what ignites the fires of present day anti-Semitism. How do we answer this? If Jews are actually the chosen people, what does that make Gentiles—second class citizens? Let's take a moment to look into this matter of chosenness.

God's sovereignty is expressed in one way through the choices He makes. There were twelve tribes of Israel and God chose one of those tribes—the tribe of Levi—to serve in the function as priests to the other eleven. We do not see the eleven tribes arguing with God about choosing the Levites as His representatives to them. Questioning God's choice would have been to question His wisdom— breaching God's authority over the nation as a whole. God not only chose Levi to represent Him to the other tribes of Israel, He also chose the twelve tribes as a whole—the nation of Israel—to represent Him as priests to the entire world: "And you shall be to Me a kingdom of priests and a holy nation" (Exod. 19:6).

In fact, all of the other nations of the world would somehow be directly linked to the priestly nation, Israel: "When the Most High divided their inheritance to the nations, when He separated the sons of Adam, He set the boundaries of the peoples according to the number of the children of Israel. For the Lord's portion is His people; Jacob is the place of His inheritance" (Deut. 32:8–9).

This is the pattern God sets. The gentile nations of the world were to draw their moral law and His divine attributes from Israel:

Many people shall come and say, "Come, and let us go up to the mountain of the Lord, to the house of the God of Jacob; He will teach us His ways and we shall walk in His paths." For out of Zion shall go forth the law, and the Word of the Lord from Jerusalem (Isa. 2:3).

For Zion's sake I will not hold My peace, and for Jerusalem's sake I will not rest, until her righteousness goes forth as brightness, and her salvation as a lamp that burns. The Gentiles shall see your righteousness, and all kings your glory. You shall be called by a new name, which the mouth of the Lord will name (Isa. 62:1–2).

I have set watchmen on your walls, O Jerusalem; they shall never hold their peace day or night. You who make mention of the Lord, do not keep silent, and give Him no rest till He establishes and till He makes Jerusalem a praise in the earth (Isa. 62:6–7).

But you shall be named the priests of the Lord, they shall call you the servants of our God (Isa. 61:6).

America has received wonderful benefit from the priestly role of Israel. Our entire judicial system is based on the ethical and moral laws of the priestly nation of Israel. As well, when it comes to knowing who the One true God is, all of our understanding of Him comes through Israel. It was the Jews who persevered for us the promises and the covenants. In fact, the Bible as a whole (possibly excluding the book of Luke) was written by the Hebrews.

One of the founding fathers of America, John Adams, wrote these words in a letter to F.A. Van der Kemp: "I will insist that the Hebrews have done more to civilize men than any other nation.... If I were an atheist....I should believe that chance had ordered the

Jews to preserve and to propagate to all mankind the doctrine of a supreme, intelligent, wise, almighty sovereign of the universe, which I believe to be the great essential principle of all morality, and consequently, of all civilization."[1]

When God made His covenant with Abraham He declared: "I will bless those who bless you, and I will curse him who curses you; and in you all the families of the earth shall be blessed" (Gen. 12:3).

God has kept that covenant through Abraham's seed, and today the entire world has been blessed by these uniquely chosen people. Consider the words of Leslie Flynn in his book, *What the Church Owes the Jew*:

> If an anti-Semite decided to boycott all the tests and cures discovered by the Jews, he would certainly open himself to a host of serious diseases. Besides refusing Jonas Salk's polio Vaccine, he would also decline the polio pill by Dr. Albert Sabin; the test to fight diphtheria invented by Bela Schick; the diet regime of Joseph Goldberger which has fought pellagra to a stand-still; blood transfusion made possible by the work of Dr. E. J. Cohen of Harvard...the Wasserman test for syphilis; the vaccine for hepatitis discovered by Baruch Blumberg; streptomycin discovered by Dr. Selman Abraham Waxman as an antibiotic; ...chlorohydrate for convulsions discovered by Dr. J. Von Liebig; and vitamins discovered by Casimir Funk.[2]

Something else that is interesting to note is that between 1901 and 2008, twenty-three percent of all individual recipients of the Nobel Prize were Jewish. These awards were given in the fields of chemistry, economics, medicine, and physics. In the same period, thirty-seven percent of all U.S. recipients of the Nobel Prize were Jewish. What makes this of note is the fact that only a quarter of a percent of the world's population and only two percent of the U.S. population is Jewish. The Jews are simply fulfilling their role as a servant/priest nation to the world and offering themselves as a blessing to mankind. Although they are blinded to Messiah their servant role has not changed.

Nowhere in the Scriptures does this chosenness mean superiority over other nations or peoples. God did not choose Israel because of her stature among the other nations. Indeed, she was the smallest and weakest of all the nations: "The Lord did not set His love on you nor choose you because you were more in number than any other people, for you were the least of all peoples; But because the Lord loves you, and because He would keep the oath which He swore to your fathers, the Lord has brought you out with a mighty hand and redeemed you from the house of bondage, from the hand of Pharaoh king of Egypt" (Deut. 7:7–8).

Here we see exactly why God chose the Hebrews: they were descendants of Abraham to whom God made a covenant ("because He would keep the oath which He swore to your fathers") because of Abraham's belief in the One true God. Abraham believed God, so God chose him and his descendants to represent Him in the earth. How God would deal with the Hebrews through history—in blessings, covenants, severity, and judgment would be an example to all the nations.

What has this chosenness meant for the Jew? Has it brought great privilege and elitism? By no means! Since their inception as a family and as a nation under Moses, the Jews have carried a heavy burden. Under the mighty hand of Him who did the choosing they have (with continual suffering) sojourned through history in a pattern of righteousness, sin, judgment, scattering among the nations, repentance, return, and restoration: "You only have I known of all the families of the earth; Therefore I will punish you for all your iniquities" (Amos 3:2).

This is the Hebrew people's long enduring history with God. Because of this, it is not uncommon to hear these words spoken from the mouth of a Jew: "Oh Lord, I know we are the chosen people, but every once in a while could you choose someone else?" From the outset of God's choice of this people they became His standard bearer—His example—of both His judgment upon sin and His wonderful mercy and blessing. Yet, because of a misperception of this divine choice of the Jews through history, the gentile church has in many quarters refused to honor the infinite wisdom of God in making this choice because of a deep seeded jealousy. In reality, if the gentile church over the ages had actually understood what being a chosen standard bearer meant, they would have wanted no part of it. Remember, the people that have shed the most blood and endured the most suffering for their faith in the God of Abraham has been the Jews. Yet, many gentile Christians continue to question God's sovereign choice. Paul addresses God's sovereign will in Romans 9: "But indeed, O man, who are you to reply against God? Will the thing formed say to him who formed it, 'Why have you made me like this?' Does not the potter have power over the clay?...'" (Rom. 9:20–21).

In disregarding God's choice, some have tried to blur the lines between Jewish and gentile distinctiveness. They interpret passages like these to mean all Christians become Jews at salvation: "There is neither Jew nor Greek [Gentile], there is neither slave nor free, there is neither male nor female, for you are all one in Christ Jesus" (Gal. 3:28).

Is this true? Are all gentile Christians Jews? Do all males become females when they are saved? Do all females become males? What then is Paul saying here? He is saying in Jesus we are one, but we do not lose our unique distinctiveness. A male and female do not lose their masculine and feminine distinctiveness when they come to Jesus. They are two completely different people physically and emotionally. But spiritually they are one in Jesus. Yet, even so, they have different spiritual callings. In a husband and wife relationship the husband is to be the spiritual covering of his wife and children. This is his distinctive role. As he spiritually nurtures and blesses his wife she is free to express her Proverbs 31 gifting in the family and community. She is a spiritually covered woman with her own special calling and anointing. Man and wife, male and female, are equal in Messiah but have different roles. It is the same with Jews and Gentiles. Jews are people who are blood descendants of Abraham. Their role is to be a nation of priests to the world. Gentile Christians are people who God has called out of the nations to become a people for His Name. Their role is to be a servant priest nation that makes the Jew jealous unto salvation. Spiritually, Gentiles are also of the seed of Abraham: "And if you are Christ's, then you are Abraham's seed, and heirs according to the promise" (Gal. 3:29).

Praise be to God! Gentiles, through the Spirit of adoption have been born into the family of God. We now share in all of the covenant blessings as Abraham seed! We are equal with Jews and joint heirs with Jews, yet we have two distinct callings. Just what would happen if all Gentiles became Jews upon their salvation? What if we lost our distinctive calling? The Jews would never be provoked to jealousy unto salvation by a righteous gentile remnant of saints who have been chosen by God for that very purpose! If Jews are never provoked to jealousy by believing Gentiles and come to Messiah, then Jews and Gentiles will never become one new man in Messiah. As a result, the world cannot be reconciled to God. This is why Paul the Jew became an apostle to the Gentiles. He knew their obedience to their distinct calling was the key to Israel bearing fruit in salvation and ultimately to the harvest of the world.

When Jesus prayed His high priestly prayer in John 17 that Jew and Gentile would be one in Him, He was not praying that their unique callings would be erased. He was praying that they would bring their distinctiveness to a mutually dependant relationship and walk in unity as one body in Messiah. The apostle Peter makes this very clear in his letter to mainly gentile believers: "But you are a chosen generation, a royal priesthood, a holy nation, His own special people, that you may proclaim the praises of Him who called you out of darkness into His marvelous light; who once were not a people but are now the people of God, who had not obtained mercy but now have obtained mercy" (1 Pet. 2:9–10).

The Gentiles are now a chosen people. They have a special calling, and that is to proclaim praise to God for making them a people—part of the commonwealth of Israel—the people of God. As we saw in our last chapter, this declaration of praise by a nation that was not a nation and a people that was not a people—together with Jewish believers in Messiah—is the key that bombards and opens the heavens for the last great move of God upon planet earth! For the praise to express the power of God to reconcile two people with such historical enmity it must be sung by both Jew and Gentile together as one! Dear gentile saint, this is our calling and mandate. If we blur the lines and lose our distinctiveness we cannot proclaim the wisdom of God in reconciling the world to Himself by restoring the relationship between these two distinct peoples.

Jewish believers who have had the blinders taken away are aware of their role as servant priests to the Gentiles. They know the desire God has for the nations to be saved. Look what God Himself says about His deep love and compassion for Gentiles who desire to come into fellowship with Him: "Do not let the son of the foreigner who has joined himself to the Lord speak, saying, 'the Lord has utterly separated me from His people'; nor let the eunuch say, 'here I am, a dry tree.' For thus says the Lord: 'To the eunuchs who keep My Sabbaths, and choose what please Me, and hold fast My covenant, even to them I will give in My house and within my walls a place and a name better than that of sons and daughters; I will give them an everlasting name that shall not be cut off'" (Isa. 56:3–5).

So, this is God's choice: Israel was chosen as a light to the nations of the world:

Many nations shall come and say, "Come, and let us go up to the mountain of the Lord, to the house of the God of Jacob; He will teach us His ways, and we shall walk in His paths." For out of Zion the law shall go forth and the word of the Lord from Jerusalem (Mic. 4:2).

Thus says the Lord of hosts: In those days ten men from every language of the nations shall grasp the sleeve of a Jewish man, saying, "Let us go with you, for we have heard that God is with you" (Zech. 8:23).

One day, the government of the world will be upon the shoulders of King Jesus. The nations will despise the nation of Israel and the King who rules from within her gates (Ps. 2:1–6). Presently, national Israel has been reborn. Yes, the nation is humanistic and her glory has not yet returned. But this is the way God works: first the natural and then the spiritual. The fact that Israel has been reborn after 1,900 years of dispersion is nothing short of miraculous. It is because of God's everlasting covenant with that people. Even when they are faithless He remains faithful. You can be sure that spiritual Israel will soon follow.

How should we respond to a people that carried the burden of bringing God to the world? Again, more than any other people, the Hebrews have shed the most blood for their belief in the God of Abraham, Isaac, and Jacob. Because of the world's hatred and rebellion towards the God they represent, the priest nation of Hebrews has been driven like lambs to the slaughter throughout history. Knowing their final restoration is recorded in the pages of the Bible, do we love them now even in their blindness? Yes! All the more because of their blindness! Remember, it was through their blindness that God opened the door to the Gentiles: "For as you were once disobedient to God, yet have now obtained mercy through their disobedience, even so these also have now been disobedient, that through the mercy shown you they also may obtain mercy. For God has committed them all to disobedience, that He might have mercy on all" (Rom. 11:30–32). With humble and grateful hearts, it is the mandate of gentile believers to honor the unique calling of Israel that will culminate in a future restoration.

Honor

For centuries the church has believed God's choice of Israel meant superiority rather than servanthood. Out of jealousy the church has taken the role of "chosen" for itself. The only way to prove its hierarchy over and above the Jew has been to segregate them in ghettos and then drive them from cities, or worse yet extinguish them. Instead of being a sign to us of a doorway into salvation, their blindness has been an excuse for persecution and dishonor.

Jeremiah the prophet speaks of this dishonor: "Have you not considered what these people have spoken saying, 'The two families which the Lord has chosen [Israel and Judah], He has also cast them off'?' Thus they have despised My people, as if they should no more be a nation before them" (Jer. 33:24).

Yet, the Jew is still here. They are a nation once again. They still carry the burden of Choice. The fact that this is so—that the Jew still exists and is presently being reborn in their own land—is what vexes the anti-Jew. Really though, are those who hate the Jews and want to divide their land ultimately angry with modern Israel? Actually, it is much deeper than that. At the core of present Christian anti-Semitism is a dishonor of God's choice. It is not Israel itself that brings the divide, but the One who chose Israel. The argument is not with Israel but with the God of Israel for His choice of Israel.

To disregard God's divine choice of this people and this land, is to despise the choice as a foolish and distasteful thing. In reality, this is to despise God. Debating God's choice of Israel is to loudly proclaim that one cannot live under God's sovereign rule. Arguing with God over the issue of Israel discloses the dark rebellion of a person's heart. If one dishonors God's divine wisdom they dishonor Him in everything. This is why for centuries Ephesians 3:10–11 has yet to be fulfilled in most church circles: "...to the intent that now the manifold wisdom of God might be made known by the church to the principalities and powers in the heavenly places, according to the eternal purpose which He accomplished in Christ Jesus our Lord."

The church cannot make an open declaration of God's wisdom to the principalities and powers if we ultimately question the choice that emanated from His wisdom. Our present mandate is to honor God's divine choice by honoring the people whom He chose. Our very salvation came as a result of that sovereign choice ("salvation is of the Jews" [John 4:22]), and our response should be gratefulness and honor rather than jealousy. The hour has come for us to honor our spiritual fathers of the faith. On God's prophetic time clock that set time coincides with a time in which Israel is being rebuilt and reborn:

167

You will arise and have mercy on Zion; for the time to favor her, yes, the set time has come. For your servants take pleasure in her stones, and show favor to her dust. So the nations shall fear the name of the Lord, and all the kings of the earth Your glory. For the Lord shall build up Zion; He shall appear in His glory. He shall regard the prayer of the destitute, and shall not despise their prayer. This will be written for the generation to come, that a people yet to be created may praise the Lord (Ps. 102:13–18).

David says that right before the appearing of the Lord in glory, Jerusalem will be built up. As the city is reborn, a people that did not yet exist in David's day will proclaim: "The set time to favor Zion has come"! They will take pleasure in her stones and in her land. This new people—the righteous remnant of saved Gentiles from the nations—will honor God's sovereign choice of the people and the land of Israel.

The Fathers

In speaking of the Jewish people, Paul says in Romans 11:28–29: "Concerning the gospel they are enemies for your sake, but concerning the election they are beloved for the sake of the fathers. For the gifts and the calling of God are irrevocable."

God honors the Jewish nation today and calls them "beloved." Even though their glory has departed and they are blind to the Messiah they are still His beloved. He loves them because He made a covenant with their fathers. He is a covenant keeping God. He made covenants with the Jewish fathers—the patriarchs of Israel—and He will never break His covenants. Even Jesus came as a servant to the Jews because of God's covenant with the fathers: "Now I say that Jesus Christ has become a servant to the circumcision [Jews] for the truth of God, to confirm the promises made to the fathers" (Rom. 15:8).

This is the hour to favor Zion. The set time has come. God is restoring the hearts of the fathers (our Hebraic heritage) to the children (gentile believers) (Mal. 4:6). Out of allegiance to the God of the Hebrews who made a covenant with Israel, and out of honor to the fathers with whom He established that covenant, we now must (as Jesus did) in humility serve the Jewish people. For the sake of the fathers we love them. For the sake of Jesus we serve them because they are His brethren. And, as we serve them we are serving Jesus: "Inasmuch as you did it to one of the least of these My brethren, you did it to Me" (Matt. 25:40). For the sake of the fathers—the biblical patriarchs of old, the Lord is drawing the Jewish people back to their own land where He will ultimately restore them: "Therefore prophesy and say to them, 'Thus says the Lord God: Behold, O My people, I will open your graves and cause you to come up from your graves, and bring you into the land of Israel...I will put My Spirit in you, and you shall live, and I will place you in your own land. Then you shall know that I, the Lord, have spoken it and performed it.' Says the Lord" (Ezek. 37:12, 14).

One day in the future all the nations of the earth will rise against the tiny nation of Israel (Zech. 12:3). The rebellion against God's choice and His priest nation will culminate in a satanic frenzy led by the Antichrist. During that time, God Himself will defend the inhabitance of Jerusalem and destroy the nations that rise against her. In Israel's future misery, will there be a righteous remnant of Gentiles from the nations who will shelter, feed, and minister to her in her hour of need? Do righteous Gentiles play a role in the end-time restoration of Israel? Do righteous Gentiles have an appointment with Israel in the wilderness? You will find the answers to these questions in our next chapter but first a word about Israel's final restoration and redemption: "And I will pour on the house of David and on the inhabitants of Jerusalem the Spirit of grace and supplication; then they will look on Me whom they pierced. Yes, they will mourn for Him as one mourns for his only son, and grieve for Him as one grieves for a firstborn....In that day a fountain shall be opened for the house of David and for the inhabitants of Jerusalem, for sin and for uncleanness" (Zech. 12:10; 13:1).

We anticipate this great day! May we honor God's choice of Israel and pray for her soon restoration. May we call her "beloved" for the sake of the Hebrew fathers of our faith with whom God made a covenant. Like many in the church throughout history, may we pray for the peace of Jerusalem, take pleasure in her stones and show favor even to her dust! The two minute warning alarm has sounded. The set time to favor Zion has come! The revolution of restoration is here! It is time for Jew and Gentile as one to proclaim the wisdom of God: "Oh God, break through the principalities and powers of the heavenly realm. Through the reconciliation of Jew and Gentile in Messiah, may You reconcile all things to Yourself: things in heaven, things on earth, and things under the earth! We look forward to that day! Even so come quickly Lord Jesus!" May the words of this historic hymn sound the two minute warning in our hearts:

Wake, harp of Zion, wake again,
Upon thine ancient hill,
On Jordan's long deserted plain,
By Kedron's lowly rill.
The hymn shall yet in Zion swell
That sounds Messiah's praise,
And Thy loved name, Immanuel!
As once in ancient days,
For Israel yet shall own her King,
For her salvation waits,
And hill and dale shall sweetly sing
With praise in all her gates.
Hasten, O Lord, these promised days,
When Israel shall rejoice;
And Jew and Gentile join in praise,
With one united voice.

James Edmeston, 1846

PART III:

The Revolution of Preparation

The Story of
Le Chambon–Sur–Lignon

We must take sides. Neutrality helps the oppressor,
never the victim. Silence encourages the tormenter,
never the tormented. Sometimes we must interfere.
Elie Wiesel

In the sleepy mountains of southeastern France rests the village
of Le Chambon-Sur-Lignon. During the Nazi occupation of France,
Le Chambon numbered almost five thousand people, mainly of the
Protestant French Huguenot tradition.

Historians are baffled over the activities of these villagers during
the occupation. Throughout Christian Europe during the Holocaust,
Jews were sheltered by many individual well meaning Christians.
However, there is little evidence of church congregations or Christian organizations within the Nazi occupied areas who were corporately involved in the rescue of Jews. On the contrary, as we have
already seen, when given the opportunity to turn in the names of

Jews to the Nazis, Christians were quick to comply—sometimes even betraying Jewish believers within their own congregations. In France alone, eighty-three thousand Jews were delivered by their Christian neighbors to the death camps—among them were ten thousand children.

In this way, the village of Le Chambon-Sur-Lignon stands alone as the largest group of Christians who worked together to protect Jews from certain death in the gas chambers. It is interesting that a mountain hamlet filled with simple, salt of the earth people, would risk their lives in order to shield the chosen. More remarkably, each family within the village took Jews into their own homes. If one member of the community informed the Nazi authorities of the villager's activities, the entire population of townspeople would have been executed.

Pastor Andre Trocme

Led by their pastor, Andre Trocme and his wife Magda, these simple Christians gave refuge for several years to nearly five thousand Jewish men, women, and children—an astounding number. In their years of evasive activity, several members of the village were arrested. For their kindness to the Jews they were murdered by the Nazis. One of these Christian martyrs was Pastor Trocme's cousin, Daniel Trocme. He was a teacher in the village school and was sheltering five Jewish students. The students were sent to Auschwitz where they died, and Daniel was deported to Lublin Mandanek concentration camp where he died. Another martyr was the Physician of Le Chambon, Dr. Roger Le Forestier. He was instrumental in preparing false documents for Jews in order to help them escape into Switzerland. Dr. Forestier was arrested on August 20, 1944 and shot by order of the Gestapo in Lyon.

A former child refugee in Le Chambon, Elizabeth Koenig-Kaufman, had this to say about her experience in the village: "Nobody asked who was Jewish and who was not. Nobody asked where you were from. Nobody asked who your father was or if you could pay. They just accepted each of us, taking us in with warmth, sheltering children, often without their parents—children who cried in the night from nightmares."[1]

The entire village of Le Chambon-Sur-Lignon has been inducted into the Yad Vashem Holocaust memorial in Jerusalem—being given the title of Righteous Among the Nations. They were afforded this honor because of their humanitarianism and bravery in the face of peril and death.

Pierre Sauvage

Pierre Sauvage was one of the Jewish children saved by the believers of Le Chambon. He has produced a film called Weapons of the Spirit. The film chronicles the epic story of the Huguenots of Le Chambon. In a speech given at the U.S. Holocaust Memorial Council Conference in Washington D.C. on September 19, 1984, Pierre explains why he believes this village of righteous gentile Christians responded towards the Jews in the way they did—especially when other communities in Christian Europe were sending Jews to their death. Here are the opening lines to Pierre's speech:

One day fifty years ago, a young French pastor arrived with his wife and children in what seemed to these cosmopolitan city people a rather sleepy mountain community. The new parish had, however, one promising feature, which the pastor, Andre Trocme, described in a letter to an American friend. In Le Chambon-Sur-Lignon, Trocme wrote, "the old Huguenot spirit is still alive. The humblest peasant home has its Bible and the father reads it every day. So these people who do not read the papers but the Scriptures do not stand on the moving soil of opinion but on the rock of the Word of God."

Time would soon prove just how right he was.

In the speech, Pierre Sauvage asks ten piercing questions about the nature of the rescuers in Le Chambon-Sur-Lignon. The questions are all the more challenging because Pierre is Jewish. Listed below are two of the questions he poses:

1. Given that the Holocaust occurred in the heart of Christian Europe and would not have been possible without the apathy or complicity of most Christians and without the virulent tradition of anti-Semitism that had long infested the very soul of Christianity, are we nonetheless to view these Christians of Le Chambon and other caring Christians of that time as rare but legitimately representative embodiments of exemplary Christian faith or merely as marginal, possibly accidental successes of a disastrously ineffective one?

2. Where were their distinctive religious attitudes and perceptions? What did the peasants and villagers of Le Chambon understand that so tragically eluded their Christian brethren? Could it be, for instance, that the righteous Christians were, in particular, Christians who were comfortable with the Jewish roots of their faith, indeed with the Jewishness of Jesus? Were they Christians for whom Christianity was, perhaps, more the religion of Jesus than the religion about Jesus? This appears to have been remarkably the case in Le Chambon, where a number of Jews never got over their astonishment at being not only sheltered but welcomed as the People of God, and where Judaism was sheltered to some extent and not just persecuted people who happened to have been Jews.

The Revolution of Preparation

Such is the story of Le Chambon-Sur-Lignon. When faced with the persecution of Jews, these righteous Gentiles risked their lives to save them. In the coming days, each of us will have our chance to respond in the same way as the good people of Le Chambon. There is a third revolution that is already approaching and it is called the revolution of preparation. The world will grow ever more vengeful in its quest to eradicate Jews from the earth. A second holocaust is already brewing in the wings. The Lord, in His great mercy towards His chosen people is preparing an army of righteous gentile believers who are preparing now to minister to them in their suffering. In this chapter and the next, we will discuss the biblical mandate to prepare mercy ministries for the Jewish people. Noah received a warning from the Lord concerning the impending doom of a world-wide flood: "By faith Noah, being divinely warned of things not yet seen, moved with godly fear, PREPARED an ark for the saving of his household, by which he condemned the world and became heir of the righteousness which is according to faith" (Heb. 11:7).

Like Noah, we understand from Scripture that cataclysmic changes are about to take place in our world. Jesus told us in Matthew 24:6–13:

And you will hear of wars and rumors of wars. See that you are not troubled; for all these things must come to pass, but the end is not yet. For nation will rise against nation, and kingdom against kingdom. And there shall be famines, pestilences, and earthquakes in various places. All these are the beginning of sorrows. Then they will deliver you up to tribulation and kill you, and you will be hated by all nations for My name's sake. And then many will be offended, will betray one another, and will hate one another. Then many false prophets will rise up and deceive many. And because lawlessness will abound the love of many will grow cold. But he who endures to the end shall be saved.

Facing impending worldwide tribulation, Noah acted proactively and "moved with godly fear" and "prepared an ark for the saving of his household." Jesus said that "as the days of Noah were, so also will the coming of the Son of Man be" (Matt. 24:37). In our day there will be men and women—modern-day Noahs—who will have understanding concerning the things to come and prepare an "ark" for the saving of many people. This ark will look entirely different than Noah's. It will consist of a worldwide infrastructure of humanitarian aid specifically prepared to aid Jews during the coming holocaust against them.

We have discovered so far that in the coming days, the nation of Israel will be completely cut off and separated from the world community. Eventually, all of the nations of the earth will seek to divide and destroy Israel: "And it shall happen in that day that I will make Jerusalem a very heavy stone for all peoples; all who would heave it away will surely be cut in pieces, though all nations of the earth are gathered against it" (Zech. 12:3; see also Joel 3:2). In direct response to this worldwide rejection of God's covenant people, there will be an ongoing restoration in the relationship between gentile and Jewish believers in Jesus. This righteous remnant of gentile saints will join themselves in solidarity not only with the Messianic believing Jews but with the nation of Israel as a whole. Thus, these two coming revolutions (separation and restoration) will happen simultaneously.

As engrafted branches, do we have any other choice but to unite ourselves with Israel? God has one olive tree, not two. The personal cost to the Gentile for such committed solidarity with Jews in a time of persecution will be high. This is why only the authentic righteous remnant will choose a path such as this. In the coming future holocaust against the Jews, these righteous Gentiles will put their own lives on the line in order to serve their elder Jewish brothers and sisters. They will fulfill the words of Jesus in Matthew 25:31–40:

When the Son of man comes in all of His glory, and all the holy angels with Him, then He will sit on the throne of His glory. All the nations will be gathered before Him, and He will separate them one from another, as a shepherd divides his sheep from the goats. And He will set the sheep on His right hand, but the goats on the left. Then the King will say to those on His right hand, "Come, you blessed of My Father, inherit the kingdom prepared for you from the foundation of the world: for I was hungry and you gave Me food; I was thirsty and you gave Me drink; I was a stranger and you took Me in; I was naked and you clothed Me; I was sick and you visited Me; I was in prison and you came to Me." Then the righteous will answer Him, saying, "Lord, when did we see You hungry and feed you, or thirsty and give You drink? When did we see You a stranger and take You in, or naked and clothe You? Or when did we see You sick, or in prison, and come to You?" And the King will answer and say to them,

"Assuredly, I say to you, inasmuch as you did it to one of the least of these My brethren, you did it to Me."

As we have already seen, the "brethren" that Jesus mentions here are Jewish people. Jesus was born a Jew, lived as a Jew, died as a Jew, was buried as a Jew, and rose from the dead—still Jewish. In fact, He's still very Jewish today. Matthew 25 is Christ's message concerning the end of the age. Jesus is saying that during the final moments of history, His "brethren" the Jews will be imprisoned, homeless, naked, hungry, and thirsty. However, a group of people that Jesus calls "the righteous" will have mercy on the Jews and protect, nourish, and comfort them in their distress.

Are Your Lamps Trimmed with Oil?

Regardless of your particular view of when the rapture occurs, we believe it is shortsighted and risky to be unprepared for the final quarter. We find it shocking that most Christians seem unconcerned about the endgame. Instead of proclaiming preparedness, watchfulness, vigilance, and soberness, it seems that the body of Christ in recent years has grown weary in waiting for the Lord's return. Like the ten virgins in Matthew 25, it seems that we have all fallen asleep on our watch. Brothers and sisters, please don't leave the final pages of your playbook blank! Prepare yourselves and your family for earth's coming night, however long it may last. How can we base the safety and protection of our family on a theory that has not yet been proven? Just what if the Lord has chosen to deliver us "through" not "out of" the Tribulation period?

An End-Time Scenario

Here is an end-time scenario that you may not have heard before. It has to do with our appointment with Israel in the wilderness (should we enter the Tribulation period). We can assure you this scenario is not for the fainthearted. The issue of Israel, the Jew, and the believing gentile remnant is the central theme of the end-times. Jesus was talking about His Jewish brethren when He said in Matthew 25:40: "Inasmuch as you did it to [feed, clothe, and shelter] one of the least of these My brethren, you did it to Me." Our love and concern for the Jew in distress is really a mirrored image of our love for Christ. To reject the last days suffering Jew, Jesus says, is to reject Him. To hate the Jew is to hate Christ. To persecute the Jew is to persecute Christ. This burden-bearing intense mercy or equally intense distaste of the Jew in his rejected plight Jesus speaks of in Matthew 25, will forever distinguish the line between the apostolic and apostate church of the last days.

A new holocaust is emerging out of the putrid nostrils of demon spirits that will hunt the Jew down the world over. One only has to look at the present anti-Jewishness of radical Islam and the rise of the thousands of acts of violence against Jews in countries like France, Britain, Germany, and Belgium, to discover that a new anti-Semitism is on the rise. As in the final solution created in the twisted minds of the Nazi SS in World War II, the Jews will once again seek refuge from slaughter. What nation will stand with them? What port of entry will receive their ships filled with desperate refugees? Who will dare give them sanctuary? If we forget history, history is bound to be repeated. If we run from history it will catch up to us.

The SS St. Louis

Let's not forget the plight of the nearly one thousand Jews aboard the SS St. Louis that left Hamburg, Germany on May 13, 1939, bound for Cuba. The Jews were escaping the Nazi regime that had already begun evacuating their people to the concentration camps. This journey to Cuba promised safe sanctuary and a hope for the evacuees to later receive visas into the United States. The plight of these refugees gained worldwide attention when the ship arrived in Havana harbor and was ordered not to dock. During the ship's voyage the

Cuban government had passed a resolution denying visas to Jewish refugees. After several days of negotiations with Cuban officials, the ship was turned back out to sea still carrying its human cargo. Before heading back to Germany, the *St. Louis* skirted the Florida coast for five days hoping against hope that the United States government would give the Jews haven and save the men, women, and children who faced an uncertain future should they be forced back to Europe. Though negotiations with U.S. immigration officials were held, no welcome to the fleeing Jews was ever issued and the ship returned to Germany. History records that over 500 people on board the *St. Louis* would later perish in the gas chambers.

The book *Night* by Elie Wiesel is the gripping story of Wiesel's experience in the German concentration camps Auschwitz and Buchenwald during the Holocaust. Wiesel was fifteen when he was deported with his family from their home in Sighet, Transylvania, in 1944. His parents and little sister all perished in the ovens. Elie reminds us never to forget the Holocaust: "To forget would be not only dangerous but offensive; to forget the dead would be akin to killing them a second time...there is 'response' in responsibility. When we speak of this era of evil and darkness, so close and yet so distant, 'responsibility' is the key word. The witness has forced himself to testify. For the youth of today, for the children who will be born tomorrow. He does not want his past to become their future."[2]

On December 10, 1986, Elie Wiesel received the Nobel Peace Prize in Oslo, Norway. In his acceptance speech he had this to say: "And that is why I swore never to be silent whenever and wherever human beings endure suffering and humiliation. We must take sides. Neutrality helps the oppressor, never the victim. Silence encourages the tormentor, never the tormented. Sometimes we must interfere. When human lives are endangered, when human dignity is in jeopardy, national borders and sensitivities become irrelevant. Human suffering anywhere concerns men and woman everywhere. Our lives no longer belong to us alone; they belong to all those who need us desperately."[3]

The Daring Saints of the Last Days

Like the residents of Le Chambon-Sur-Lignon who sheltered Jews during the Holocaust, will there be such daring saints in the last days that will risk their lives in order to protect God's covenant people? During the end-times, the vile hatred of the Jew will culminate in their being driven into the wilderness by the Antichrist himself—the man of lawlessness, the man of sin. Wise gentile believers who understand the coming plight of world Jewry will begin now to prepare an infrastructure for the saving of many people.

Like Noah, this godly righteous remnant will prepare food, water, and shelter for Jews in flight. Like Joseph who built storehouses of grain for the coming famine, these gentile Christians will be modern-day deliverers. A reading of Revelation 12 describes our appointment in the wilderness with the Jews: "The woman [The Jewish nation] fled into the wilderness, where she has a place PREPARED by God, that they [righteous Gentiles?] should feed her there one thousand two hundred and sixty days....But the woman was given two wings of a great eagle, that she might fly into the wilderness to her place, where she is nourished [by righteous Gentiles?] for a time and times and half a time, from the presence of the serpent" (Rev. 12:6, 14; see also Isa. 16:2–4; Ezek. 20:35; Hosea 2:14–15).

In the coming dark days, if we choose to become the righteous remnant that Jesus speaks of in Matthew 25, and give sanctuary to the persecuted Jew, it could bring about our own suffering. For some, to love the Jew in their plight and join in their suffering may prove too difficult. However, it may be the one and only thing that fulfills Romans 11:11: "I say, then, have they [Jewish people] stumbled that they should fall? Certainly not! But through their fall, to provoke them to jealousy, salvation has come to the Gentiles."

The very reason why God grafted Gentiles into the olive tree (the root system of Abraham, Isaac, and Jacob) was to provoke the Jew to jealousy that they might be grafted back in again! What greater thing could provoke an unbelieving Jew to a jealousy that brings them to Jesus their Messiah than a righteous remnant of gentile Christians willing to risk their lives to nourish and protect them? The Bible is filled with passages that describe this righteous remnant of Christians from the nations of the world who have prepared an "ark" of mercy and protection for the Jews of the last days. Isaiah the prophet describes this ministry of mercy performed by righteous Gentiles:

Behold, I will lift My hand in an oath to the nations [these are gentile nations], and set up My standard for the peoples; they shall bring your sons in their arms, and your daughters shall be carried on their shoulders; kings shall be your foster fathers, and their queens your nursing mothers" (Isa. 49:22–23).

Gentiles shall come to your light, and kings to the brightness of your rising. Lift up your eyes all around, and see; they all gather together, they come to you; your sons shall come from afar and your daughters shall be nursed at your side....the wealth of the Gentiles shall come to you...the sons of foreigners shall build up your walls, and their kings shall minister to you...you shall drink the milk of the Gentiles, and milk the breast of kings (Isa. 60:3–4, 5, 10, 16).

Could these kings and queens from the gentile nations who nourish Israel in their distress be righteous end-time Christians? It is very possible.

A Call to Authenticity

There are many within the church today that have a great love for Jewish people. Those who love the Jewish people must presently move beyond an affinity with Jews into solidarity with them. We must set aside our romantic feelings about the nation of Israel and become authentically committed to the people of Israel—come what may. Our commitment to help the Jews—especially those in the believing community—does not replace our responsibility to evangelize other nations. Actually, the restoration of the relationship with our Jewish brothers and sisters in Christ will be the catalyst that exponentially propels the gospel to the four corners of the earth. As we saw in the introduction to this book, there are seventy-three words in the high priestly prayer of Jesus that confirm this (see John 17:20–22).

There is a beautiful passage of Scripture in Psalm 110:3: "Your people shall be volunteers in the day of Your power." In these days of uncertainty will you be part of the righteous remnant of gentile believers who will say, "Count me in! I will be a volunteer in the end-time preparation of mercy ministries to aid Jews in their future suffering?" The infrastructure of this "ark" is already being prepared through Jewish relief ministries all around the globe. The Lord Jesus is already revolutionizing His church, and saints are being awakened to His end-time purposes. Please be very cautious where you send your resources. Not every ministry that receives finances for suffering Jews is legitimate. In the words of Elie Wiesel: "Our lives no longer belong to us alone; they belong to all those who need us desperately." There is an old Jewish proverb which says: "He who saves one life saves the world entire."

The true story of Oskar Schindler was portrayed in a movie directed by Steven Spielberg, Schindler's List. Schindler, a Gentile, sacrificed his wealth and rescued over one thousand Jews from the gas chambers during the Holocaust. At the end of the movie, Schindler laments that he could have done more to save more lives. In the closing scene is this exchange between the German businessman Schindler and his Jewish bookkeeper, Itzhak Stern:

Oskar Schindler: I could've got more...I could've got more; if I'd just...I could've got more...

Stern: Oscar, there are eleven hundred people who are alive because of you. Look at them.

Schindler: If I'd made more money...I threw away so much money, you have no idea. If I'd just....

Stern: There will be generations because of what you did.

Schindler: I didn't do enough.

Stern: You did so much.

Schindler: This car, Goeth would have bought this car. Why did I keep this car? Ten people, right there. Ten people, ten more people... [He rips the swastika pin from his lapel.] This pin, two people. This is gold. Two more people. He would've given me two for it. At least one. He would've given me one. One more. One more person. A person, Stern. For this. I could've gotten one more person and I didn't. I didn't....

The Avenue of the Righteous

Courage is never alone, for it has fear as its ever-present
companion. An act deserves to be called courageous if,
and only if, it is performed in spite of fear. The greater
the fear, the more courageous the action that defies it.
Thus, it is only when fear and anxiety rule supreme that
courage can truly assert itself.

Shlomo Breznitz
*The Courage to Care: Rescuers of Jews
During the Holocaust*

If men cannot always
Make history
Have a meaning,
they can always act
so that their own lives have.

Albert Camus

At the Holocaust memorial museum in Jerusalem—Yad Vashem—there is an outdoor sunlit walkway lined with commemorate plaques. On the plaques are the names of Gentiles who risked their lives to rescue and shelter Jews during the Nazi occupation of Europe. Also lining this beautiful stone pathway are trees that have been planted in memory of these brave souls. The walkway is known as The Avenue of the Righteous of the Nations. The rescuers represent forty-two countries and nationalities. They are men and women of all ages. They are ordinary people from all walks of life and all denominations. Their occupations range from peasants to the highly educated. There were clergy, fishermen, farmers, nuns, country folk and city dwellers, university professors and school teachers. Many rescuers began as bystanders. But when they saw the unjust treatment of the Jews they got involved. Sometimes they may have simply heard a knock at their door and opened it to find a Jew on the other side asking for sanctuary. Knowing that the Jew would be killed if found in the streets they opened the door and took them in. Sometimes it was just for the night. Other times the rescuers gave shelter for months or even years. Faced with a moral decision they chose to respond.

The Time of Jacob's Trouble

In the coming days the Jewish people and the nation of Israel will enter into a period known as the Time of Jacob's trouble. This epic event will take place during the last day's Tribulation period. Jeremiah, Daniel, and Jesus speak of this harrowing space of time. Jesus says that these will be days of "great tribulation, such as has not been since the beginning of the world until this time, no, nor ever shall be" (Matt. 24:21). Listen to how Jeremiah the prophet describes it: "Alas! For that day is great, so that none is like it; and it is the time of Jacob's trouble, but he shall be saved out of it" (Jer. 30:7).

The reputation of the nation of Israel will suffer continual blows as she resorts to using unpopular methods to buoy her own survival and existence. As we saw in our last chapter, a righteous remnant of gentile saints the world over will minister to Jews with food, clothing, shelter, and medical aid. Surely, a new chapter will be written about gentile rescuers of Jews. Many will walk down the same avenue of the righteous as a Corrie Ten Boom or Oscar Schindler. Will you walk down this same pathway? Will you take the mantle of one who has already walked the avenue of the righteous?

This coming righteous remnant of gentile saints will not be caught up with self-preservation. They will not love their own lives above others. Self-gratification and self-preservation seem to be the focus of much of our world today. But it will not be so with this coming army of saints. These gentile saints will understand their critical role in drawing the Jewish nation to the Messiah, Jesus. The chosen priest/nation Israel became a servant to the world. As a people they have represented the One true God to the nations. In their attempt to breach the authority of God, the nations have historically struck down the people God has called to be His representatives. At the time of the end, Satan's furry will be unleashed in a last attempt to prevent the full restoration of Israel.

Ultimately, the objective of this cosmic struggle is to prevent the establishment of the Davidic throne and the restoration of the Kingdom whose ruler is called Faithful and True. Knowing the Kingdom is at hand and what is at stake in the conflict, righteous Gentiles will rise to the occasion. They will understand who they are in Christ and what He has called them to do. They will see themselves as a priest/nation called to be a servant to the circumcision (the Jews). They will see themselves as one with the people of God, and a vital part of the commonwealth of Israel.

Now that we understand this divine mystery, what is our response? When we are confronted and convicted by truth, it should lead to a practical response. When Paul was smitten and blinded by the light on the road to Damascus his first response was "Who are you Lord….what do you want me to do?" (Acts 9:5–6). Understanding the connection between Israel and the church in the divine mystery requires that we do something. A preparation is necessary.

The Covenant with Abraham

If you choose to heed the two minute warning and embrace the revolution of preparation, you will be in good company. The Scripture is filled with saints who carried the mantle of ministering to Jews in their weakness and suffering. These biblical gentile saints saw God's hand in choosing Israel and honored God's choice by serving His chosen. Here are a few examples of Gentiles who gave of themselves in service to Jews. Notice the promise of provision attached to each example:

In God's original covenant with Abraham He makes a promise of provision to any person or nation who would bless Abraham's descendants: "I will make you a great nation; I will bless you and make your name great; and you shall be a blessing. I will bless those who bless you, and I will curse him who curses you" (Gen. 12:2–3).

Elijah the Prophet. Elijah the Jewish prophet was hungry and thirsty. God had commanded a gentile woman to provide water and food for him. She and her son were both starving, but, out of loyalty to the mandate she received from God, she fed Elijah first. The action of this gentile woman in blessing this Jewish man opened up a supernatural door of provision as the story records:

So she said, "As the Lord your God lives, I do not have bread, only a handful of flour in a bin, and a little oil in a jar; and see, I am gathering a couple of sticks that I may go in and prepare it for myself and my son, that we may eat it, and die." And Elijah said to her, "Do not fear; go and do as you have said, but make me a small cake from it first, and bring it to me; and afterward make some for yourself and your son. For thus says the Lord God of Israel: 'The bin of flour shall not be used up, nor shall the jar of oil run dry, until the day the Lord sends rain on the earth.'" So she went away and did according to the word of Elijah; and she and he and her household ate for many days. The bin of flour was not used up, nor did the jar of oil run dry, according to the word of the Lord which He spoke by Elijah (1 Kings 17:12–16).

Cornelius. Cornelius was a centurion in the Roman city of Caesarea. He and his entire family received the Lord and were baptized in the Holy Spirit. A key that opened up a passageway in his search for God is found in the first part of his conversion story. Cornelius got God's attention because he was generously giving to the Jewish people:

There was a certain man in Caesarea called Cornelius, a centurion of what was called the Italian Regiment, a devout man and one who feared God with all his household, who gave alms generously to the people, and prayed to God always. About the ninth hour of the day he saw clearly in a vision an angel of God coming in and saying to him, "Cornelius!" And when he observed him, he was afraid and said, "what is it Lord?" So he said to him, "Your prayers and your alms have come up for a memorial before God" (Acts 10:1–4).

The Centurion in Capernaum. One of the most touching stories of the Lord providing supernaturally for a Gentile who honored and served the Jews, is the account of the centurion in the city of Capernaum: "...A certain centurion's servant, who was dear to him, was sick and ready to die. So when he heard about Jesus, he sent elders of the Jews to Him, pleading with Him to come and heal his servant. And when they came to Jesus, they begged Him earnestly, saying that the one for whom He should do this was deserving, 'for he loves our nation, and has built us a synagogue.' Then Jesus went with them" (Luke 7:2–6).

Jesus did not normally respond to Gentiles. His earthly ministry was focused on the lost sheep of Israel. Yet, here in this story he immediately responds to the need of this gentile centurion and heals his servant. Why? One simple reason: He gave of himself to the people of Capernaum out of a love for the nation of Israel. Did he see God's unique calling and election of the Jewish nation? We believe so.

A Moabitess Named Ruth.

Probably the most well known story of a Gentile who ministered to a Jewish person is the story of Ruth. Ruth was a Moabite and the daughter-in-law of Naomi, a Jewish woman. Naomi's husband and sons all died in a famine in the country of Moab leaving both she and Ruth as widows. Naomi made plans to return to Bethlehem in Israel. It would have been natural for Ruth to return to her own people, but instead she clung to Naomi and spoke these beautiful words to her mother-in-law: "Entreat me not to leave you, or to turn back from following after you; for wherever you go, I will go; and wherever you lodge, I will lodge; your people shall be my people, and your God, My God. Where you die, I will die, and there will I be buried. The Lord do so to me, and more also, if anything but death parts you and me" (Ruth 1:16–17).

The picture of this gentile woman embracing the Jew and speaking kindly to her is a powerful illustration of the present day role of gentile Christians. Ruth was saying in essence, "Count me in! I am committed to you till death. Only death itself will part me from you." These are powerfully significant words. The coming righteous gentile remnant will offer the same pledge to the Jewish people in their suffering. These gentile believers will be humble servants who will say, "Come what may—even death—I will cling to my Jewish fathers and not let go. Where they go I will go; their people will be my people, and their God, my God." Like Moses, they will reject the delicacies of Egypt in order to receive the greater riches of God's supernatural provision through Christ. These saints will be single minded and will choose to stand with the Hebrew people as Moses did even when facing affliction: "By faith Moses, when he became of age, refused to be called the son of Pharaoh's daughter, choosing rather to suffer affliction with the people of God than to enjoy the passing pleasures of sin, esteeming the reproach of Christ greater riches than the treasures in Egypt; for he looked to the reward" (Heb. 11:24–25).

Ruth returned with Naomi and served her elder Jewish mother-in-law with dedicated devotion. Ruth gleaned the fields of a relative of Naomi's named Boaz. When Boaz saw the love and tender care this gentile woman gave to Naomi, he blessed her with provision:

"Then Boaz said to Ruth, 'You will listen, my daughter, will you not? Do not go to glean in another field, nor go from here, but stay close by my young women. Let your eyes be on the field which they reap, and go after them. Have I not commanded the young men not to touch you? And when you are thirsty, go to the vessels and drink from what the young men have drawn'" (Ruth 2:8–9).

Ruth was puzzled. She questioned why she was receiving such favor from a Jewish man. In the culture of the day, she was a gentile foreigner, so to her it made absolutely no sense. But, Boaz noticed the love of this gentile woman for her Jewish mother-in-law, and it impressed him:

So she fell on her face, bowed down to the ground, and said to him, "Why have I found favor in your eyes, that you should take notice of me, since I am a foreigner?" And Boaz answered and said to her, "It has been fully reported to me, all that you have done for your mother-in-law since the death of your husband and how you have left your father and your mother and the land of your birth, and have come to a people whom you did not know before. The Lord repay your work, and a full reward be given you by the Lord God of Israel, under whose wings you have come for refuge" (Ruth 2:10–12).

Later on in the story of Ruth and Naomi, Boaz marries Ruth and redeems all of her debt. This gentile "foreigner" received abundant blessings because of her commitment to an elderly Jewish widow.

There is something else of interest to note in the Scriptures concerning the practical ministry of Gentiles to Jews. Did you know that the special offerings collected in the gentile church were given to the poor in Israel? Did you know that most of the teaching we have about giving offerings is specifically in reference to giving to poor saints in Israel? Take a look at these familiar passages:

A Humanitarian Relief Effort in Judea

The church in Antioch was made of both Jews and Gentiles. When the congregation learned of a coming famine they immediately responded by sowing finances to help the Jewish believers in Judea: "And in those days prophets came from Jerusalem to Antioch. Then one of them, named Agabus, stood up and showed by the Spirit that there was going to be a great famine throughout all the world, which also happened in the days of Claudius Caesar. Then the disciples, each according to his ability, determined to send relief to the brethren dwelling in Judea. This they also did, and sent it to the elders by the hands of Barnabas and Saul" (Acts 11:27–30).

An Offering to the Jews as a Duty

In Paul's letter to the Romans he details his plans to travel to Jerusalem and deliver to the saints there an offering from gentile churches abroad. Jewish believers in Jerusalem were not only being oppressed by Rome but by the religious Jewish leaders as well. The Gentiles felt it was their obligation to minister to their fathers of the faith. Listen to Paul's words on the matter: "But now I am going to Jerusalem to minister to the saints. For it pleased those from Macedonia and Achaia to make a certain contribution for the poor among the saints who are in Jerusalem. It pleased them indeed and they are their debtors. For if the Gentiles have been partakers of their spiritual things, their duty is also to minister to them in material things. Therefore, when I have performed this and have sealed to them this fruit, I shall go by way of you to Spain" (Rom. 15:25–28).

The Fellowship of Ministering to Jewish Believers

Prior to Paul's trip to Jerusalem he admonished the churches throughout Macedonia and Galatia to receive offerings for the poor saints living in Jerusalem. When Paul made his case to Felix in his own defense, he talks about this offering: "Now after many years I came to bring alms and offerings to my nation" (Acts 24:17). Paul spends much time in his first (1 Cor. 16:1–4) and second letter to the Corinthian gentile believers, explaining the merits of giving this offering to Jewish saints. Paul knew the price this servant/priest Jewish nation had paid to preserve the covenants and promises for the Gentiles. He also knew that the household of faith—the believing Jewish saints in Jerusalem were suffering for their belief in Jesus. The offering was to be taken to minister to the practical needs of the Jerusalem church. Paul established the priority of doing good works among the believing community first: "Therefore, as we have opportunity, let us do good to all, especially to those who are of the household of faith" (Gal. 6:10). Paul encouraged the Corinthian gentile Christians to join with the Macedonian Gentiles in a meaningful fellowship of ministering to the needs of Jewish saints in Judea:

For I bear witness that according to their [Macedonian churches] ability, yes, and beyond their ability, they were freely willing, imploring us with much urgency that we would receive the gift and the fellowship of the ministering to the saints. And not only as we had hoped, but they first gave themselves to the Lord, and then to us by the will of God….it is to your advantage, not only to be doing what you began and were desiring to do a year ago, but now you also must complete the doing of it, that as there was a readiness to desire it, so there also may be a completion out of what you have (2 Cor 8:3–5, 10).

God Loves a Cheerful Giver

Notice how Paul lays out the promise of provision that is joined to giving to Jewish saints:

Now concerning the ministering to the saints it is superfluous for me to write to you; for I know your willingness, about which I boast of you to the Macedonians, that Achaia was ready a year ago; and your zeal has stirred up the majority….But this I say: He who sows sparingly will also reap sparingly, and he who sows bountifully will also reap bountifully. So let each one give as he purposes in his heart, not grudgingly or of necessity; for God loves a cheerful giver. And God is able to make all grace abound toward you, that you, always having all sufficiency in all things, may have an abundance for every good work. As it is written: "He has dispersed abroad, He has given to the poor; His righteousness endures forever." Now may He who supplies seed to the sower, and bread for food, supply and multiply the seed you have sown and increase the fruits of your righteousness, while you are enriched in everything for all liberality, which causes thanksgiving through us to God. For the administration of this service not only supplies the needs of the saints but also is abounding through many thanksgivings to God (2 Cor. 9:1, 6–12).

The Biblical Pattern of Giving to Israel

There are many people giving to Israel today. However, not everyone is following the biblical pattern and giving first to the household of faith within Israel. Presently, there are fifteen thousand Jewish believers within congregations spread throughout the land of Israel. Many of these believers are being persecuted for their faith in Jesus. Often, Jewish believers are terminated from employment when their new faith in Jesus is discovered. Others are cut off from their families, and some have lost their citizenship. Within the believing community poverty abounds.

Yes, there are many good causes led by well meaning people, and millions of dollars have been raised to help Jews in crisis. Sadly though, these funds are generally not given to help build the believing congregations and minister to the saints. The only biblical pattern we have in giving to Jewish people is that offerings should be given to the believing saints—to the household of faith first, and then to the larger community in Israel.

Motivation in Giving

What is our motivation for giving to Israel? From the outside it looks as if American Christians are committed to Israel. Millions of dollars every year go to bless that nation. But, why are the funds given to the nation rather than the believing saints? Why are the funds not designated to build the local body of Yeshua? The answer rests in the way many view the time of the coming of the Lord.

There are three main views of when the rapture occurs: prior to the beginning of the seven year Tribulation period, in the middle, and at the very end of the Tribulation. It's interesting to note that the majority of Jewish believers in Yeshua hold to a posttribulation view. There is a reason for this: They know the history behind the other two views—especially the pretribulation rapture theory. Each one of these views is only an unproven theory. However, the pretribulation view is proclaimed as if it is a fact. But it is not a fact, only a theory. How can we proclaim something to be a fact when there is no way to prove it? Unproven pretribulationist theories have produced a false security and built an escape mentality among many Christians. The Scriptures call us to watchfulness and soberness— come what may. It seems to us that the best approach is to plan for the endgame and simply trust in the Lord's perfect timing. If the theory of a pretribulation rapture is incorrect, and Christians enter into a period of testing and trial, the faith of many will be shaken. Their trust in God will be damaged because they will conclude He failed in His promise of an early rapture. But again, no one is really sure this is actually a promise. It is one of several theories but not a promise one can be certain of.

The teaching that the church would be taken up or "raptured" before the Tribulation period begins, was made popular by a Scottish theologian named John Darby. He in turn taught the concept to American theologians. The concept has gained great strength mainly in America over the last 100 years but is not widely held as a credible view in other countries. Actually, today in many evangelical seminaries the pretribulation rapture theory is not as widely held as it once was. Because it is the most difficult of the three theories to support, it is losing ground. Much dedicated scholarship today is taking a fresh look at the posttribulation view or the prewrath view of the rapture. The prewrath view theorizes that the appearing of

Jesus—His second coming—will be right before the wrath of God is poured out at the end of the seven year Tribulation period.

The pretribulation catching away of the saints was highly criticized in the early part of its inception because at the time of the rapture a large remnant of Jews must be living in the Holy Land. In Darby's time (the last part of the 1800s) Israel had not yet become a nation. Knowing that to prove his pretribulation theory the state of Israel would need to be reborn, Darby came up with a plan. He began laying the groundwork for a movement that would help return the Jews to Israel and establish a nation there. Today, this movement is known as Christian Zionism. The motivation of this movement is to establish and protect the state of Israel at all costs. According to Christian Zionists, if Jews are not living in Israel, the pretribulation rapture of the church is in jeopardy. This is because Christian Zionists who hold to a pretribulation theology believe that the persecuted saints mentioned in Matthew 24 who reside in Israel are Jews only. As well, those enduring the fierce hatred of the Antichrist in the book of Revelation are also Jews. In order to bring about the pretribulation rapture, Christian Zionists want to help build the state of Israel and transport as many Jews as they possibly can back to the Holy Land. For them, the establishment of the state of Israel proves the theory of an early rapture of Gentiles. For them, the stronger Israel, the stronger their theory.

A Vital Missing Link

What seems to be missing here is the call to reconcile with our Messianic brothers and sisters in Yeshua so that together we can lead Jewish people to salvation. Where is the teaching of the one new man? Where is the commitment to nourish and protect Jews in their future suffering? Where is a love with no conditions or agenda? We applaud the heartfelt passion of Christian Zionists who have stood with the state of Israel. As we have seen, it was the British politician Arthur Balfour (who had roots in Christian Zionism) that played a significant role in Israel's restoration to her own land. Yet, if we support the state of Israel only because we believe its very existence guarantees our escape from tribulation, our love for the brethren of Jesus is shallow. If this is the reason why we want to help Jews return to their homeland it's as if we are once again herding them into a locked ghetto or loading them into cattle cars. Though we believe the thought is not intended to hurt Jews, it is still using the suffering of Jews to benefit gentile people looking for an early escape from tribulation. Once again, Jewish promises are taken by Gentiles while the Jews themselves are appointed to suffering. Consider the following perspective:

Starting in the 1930's the Europeans expropriated the property of their Jews and collected the physical bodies of those Jews in camps where they could be worked to death—the Nazis did not put healthy Jews into gas chambers but only those who had become exhausted by slave labor. In the 1940's and 1950's the remaining Jews of Central Europe were by and large sent to Israel while at the same time Arab nations expropriated the wealth of their 1,000 and 2,000-year-old Jewish communities and sent the physical bodies of the Jews to Israel (except for some thousands who were killed by mobs). In the last decades of the twentieth century the former Soviet Union began to export its Jewish population, though without the violence and confiscation that had accompanied Jewish migrations from Europe and Arab nations.

Historically most concentration camps for Jews have eventually turned into death camps and certainly there is no shortage of people worldwide trying to effect this transformation.[1]

We support Israel's right to defend herself. Like any other sovereign nation she has the right to self-determination. This tiny nation is surrounded by enemies that desire to annihilate her. Such has always been the case. Time and time again God has miraculously delivered Israel from her enemies. Yet, our role as gentile believers is not to militarily defend the physical borders of the nation of Israel. Our only mandate from Scripture is to minister first to the household of faith within Israel and then to the Jewish community at large—with acts of loving kindness, humanitarian aid, and the sharing of our faith in Jesus.

You might ask: "Who are the saints being persecuted during the Great Tribulation Jesus speaks of in Matthew 24? According to some Christian Zionist, Jesus is only speaking of Jews in these chapters. Think of it: while our fellow Jewish brothers and sisters are being persecuted by the false church led by the Antichrist, the gentile believers are safely taken out of the earth in a secret rapture. While multitudes of Jews are exterminated in the final holocaust against them, the church rests safely in the arms of the Jewish Messiah. Christians who hold to this view say that God will never allow His "covenant people" to endure tribulation. But, are not the Jews His covenant people as well? Not surprisingly, in the last couple of years, Jewish people have distanced themselves from Christian Zionists because they see the motivation behind their acts of mercy. This theory of the rapture, which birthed the concept of Christian Zionism, seems to us another example of long held beliefs that have divided Jews and Gentiles.

Honor and Loyalty

In terms of when the rapture will happen, the Scripture calls us to be sober minded and ready for anything—come what may. It seems to us that the more important issue is not whether gentile believers are going up in the rapture before, during, or at the end of the Tribulation. But, whether or not we are restoring the relationship with the righteous remnant of Jewish believers today. The world awaits the final harvest and the end will not come until the "gospel of the kingdom is preached in all the world as a witness to all the nations" (Matt. 24:14). According to Jesus, in His high priestly prayer in John 17, the world will come to belief only when Jewish and gentile believers become one in Messiah, Jesus.

Out of loyalty to Jesus and His Word, and out of honor for His divine choice of Israel, gentile believers should commit themselves to covenantal relationship with Jewish believers and then to the world Jewish community as a whole. True solidarity in relationship is saying to every Jew (whether or not they believe in Jesus): "We are with you, come what may! On our watch we will not allow you to be persecuted alone. When that terrible day comes we will wear the yellow patch with you!" It should not be a question of who will get an early departure from persecution but rather who will be willing to wear the yellow Star of David and rally around the Jewish people.

A larger and more serious question we would like to pose to those who support Israel based on the pretribulation rapture theory is this: What if the rapture does not happen prior to the Tribulation and you must face the coming night? Will you still be compassionate toward Jews? Are your humanitarian efforts based on solidarity and covenantal relationship or based on a theory of early escape? We are challenging the motivation behind the present frenzy in some Christian circles to romanticize Israel because her very existence proves a particular brand of eschatology. How sad. Once again the gentile church is glorified while the pitiful Jew heads to the gas chambers. We wonder if Replacement Theology has even influenced our views of the catching away of the saints.

To get around this difficult question of who the saints of the Tribulation are, some Christian Zionists have concluded that Jesus never came to be the Jewish Messiah. According to them, he was the Messiah to the Gentiles but not the Jews. Later, (after Gentiles escape in the rapture) the Jews will accept Jesus at the end of their suffering in the Tribulation. Listen to the words of one popular Christian Zionist who does not believe that Jesus came to be the Jewish Messiah:

If God intended for Jesus to be the Messiah of Israel, why didn't he authorize Jesus to use supernatural signs to prove he was God's Messiah, just as Moses had done?....Jesus refused to give a sign. He only compared himself to the prophet Jonah, who carried the message of repentance from God to the Gentiles at Nineveh. Jesus was again saying, "I have come to carry a message from God to the Gentiles...." If Jesus wanted to be Messiah, why did he repeatedly tell his disciples and followers to "tell no one" about his supernatural accomplishment? ....Why did he constantly command those who were excited about his supernatural abilities to "tell no one"? The Jews were not rejecting Jesus as Messiah; it was Jesus who was refusing to be the Messiah to the Jews.[2]

This is a very erroneous teaching. By concluding that Jesus did not come to be the Jewish Messiah, this same leader proclaims that Jews do not come to the Lord the same way that Gentiles do: "Gentiles come to Christ by the propagation of the gospel....This is not true of the Jewish people."[3]

Yet, a simple reading of Romans 9–11 describes exactly how Jews come to faith. In these three chapters Paul is talking about ministering to Jews who have been blinded to Jesus the Jewish Messiah. Does he say that proclaiming the gospel to them is futile? Listen to Paul's words: "For there is no distinction between Jew and Greek, for the same Lord over all is rich to all who call upon Him. For 'whoever calls on the name of the Lord shall be saved'" (Rom. 10:12–13).

Notice, there is no distinction between how Jews come to faith and how Gentiles come to faith! Paul now tells us exactly how both Jews and Gentiles come to the Lord: "How then shall they [remember—Paul is speaking specifically about Jewish evangelism here] call on Him in whom they have not believed? And how shall they believe in Him of whom they have not heard? And how shall they hear without a preacher? And how shall they preach unless they are sent? As it is written: 'How beautiful are the feet of those who preach the gospel of peace, who bring glad tidings of good things!'... So then faith comes by hearing, and hearing by the word of God" (Rom. 10:14–15, 17).

Jews then, come to faith through the proclamation of the Word of God in the same way as Gentiles. Why do many Christian Zionists deny this? Simply because they believe the people living in Jerusalem in Mathew 24 during the Tribulation period are unsaved Jews, not gentile Christians. If all Jews can presently be saved, there might not be enough unsaved Jews living in Israel during the Tribulation to prove a pretribulation rapture for Gentiles. Because of this belief, many Christian Zionists do not believe Jews can presently come to the Lord in large numbers. Listen again to the words of a Christian Zionist: "Some organizations who target Jewish people for conversion use the phrase from Romans 1:16, which states, 'to the Jew first,' to justify their ministry. Let's look at that whole Scripture and see what it really says: 'For I am not ashamed of the gospel of Christ, for it is the power of God to salvation for everyone who believes, for the Jew first and also for the Greek.' It's clear that the subject of this verse is the gospel of Christ. The phrase 'for the Jew first' is a matter of sequence—not preference."[4]

This Christian Zionist author seems to think it odd that "some organizations...target Jewish people for conversion." Yet, Paul the Apostle targeted Jews for evangelism. He consistently went to the synagogue and proclaimed the gospel to the Jews. Keep in mind that this was sequentially long after the gospel had been preached to the Gentiles. By this time the gospel was quickly spreading throughout the gentile world yet Paul still saw the need to proclaim the gospel to Jews. Wonderfully, he had great results. Here is one example: "Now it happened in Iconium that they went together to the synagogue of the Jews, and so spoke that a great multitude both of the Jews and of the Greeks believed" (Acts 14:1; see also Acts 13; 17:1–4; 18).

The Greatest Gift Gentile Believers Can Give

On the one hand are the Replacement Theology teachers who say: "Everything for the Jew as an individual but nothing for the Jew as a people." They don't mind Jews existing as long as they don't exist as a nation or group. Replacement thinkers do not believe that Jews have the right to self-determination as a nation of people. This is why the church (inspired by Replacement Theology) has driven the Jews out of one country or another for centuries. The church is empowering itself once again to drive the Jews not only from the nations but from the land of Israel.

On the other extreme are many Christian Zionists who believe: "Everything for the Jew as a nation but nothing for the Jew as an individual." They desire to secure the borders of Israel and help establish the secular nation of Israel but cannot accept the fact that a worldwide revival is happening among Jewish people—already conservatively numbering two hundred and fifty thousand! Why? Because if Jews come to Jesus before the rapture, it throws into question the entire teaching of pretribulation theology. So, as a result, many of our Christian Zionists friends are committed to the nation of Israel but not to the present salvation of the people of Israel. Among Christian Zionist, the subject of Jews coming to faith appears to be avoided.

We appeal to our Christian Zionist brothers and sisters. We ask you to reconsider your position on the present possibility of the salvation of Jewish people. How can anyone teach others to withhold the greatest gift we can give to the Jewish people—the presentation of Yeshua (Jesus)—their Messiah? How can anyone say that it is not yet time for Jews to come to faith? To hide this gift from Jewish people is to nullify the very purpose God called Gentiles! Shall we preach the gospel to everyone except Jews? Remember, we are the servant/priest nation that has been called to provoke Jews to a jealousy that leads them to their Messiah, Yeshua. How can we avoid this calling without jeopardizing our Intimacy with Jesus—the One who wept over them? After 1,900 years of persecuting our elder brothers we must use wisdom in how we share our faith. In many respects, one of the best ways to begin restoring Israel to her Messiah is through mercy ministries and acts of kindness. Of course, Israel's restoration to her Messiah will be realized at the Lord's appearance. But to deny them this grace in the present is a great act of betrayal.

Jesus says that in the last days His brethren the Jews will be hungry, thirsty, naked, sick, in prison, and strangers. Righteous Gentiles are called to minister to their physical needs. Yet, perhaps Jesus was also speaking here of their spiritual needs. The Jews today are spiritually hungry and thirsty. As a people they have one of the highest percentages in the world of involvement in New Age doctrine, eastern mysticism, and the occult. In Israel, secular humanism and atheism abound as the "religions" of choice among Israelis. They dwell in a spiritual vacuum—a prison—and they need deliverance. Because of the influence of secular humanism, many Jewish people the world over have become strangers to the things of God. As well, they are naked and need to be clothed with Yeshua. A blindness in part has come over this people and their eyes will soon be gloriously opened by the Lord. Could there be an end-time righteous remnant of gentile believers who will embrace the revolution of preparation and share with Jews both material and spiritual things? Yes! A thousand times yes!

We Will Not Repeat History!

It is time to begin the process of remembering. If the church fails to remember what we have done to our elder brothers over the last 1,900 years, then our past will repeat itself once again. By remembering, we have a chance to heal the divide and return to our story—a story that unites us together with Jewish believers as one. This story directly connects us to our Hebraic heritage that began with God's promises to our father Abraham. The story of Abraham and his children is our story too. The crescendo of this historical drama centers around the Jewish Messiah, Jesus. His end-time purpose is to restore Jewish and gentile believers together as one in Himself, thus opening the way to reconcile all things under His dominion and power. May we commit ourselves to this vital restoration in this hour. May the high priestly prayer of Jesus in John 17 become ours. As we saw in the introduction to this book, Jesus prayed for Jewish and gentile believers to become as one: "I do not pray for these [Jewish believers] alone, but also for those [future Gentiles] who will believe in Me through their word; that they all may be one, as You, Father, are in Me, and I in You; that they also may be one is Us, that the world may believe that You sent Me" (John 17:20–21).

The Three Revolutions Have Begun!

The Lord Jesus is now seated at the right hand of God. We believe He continues to pray the high priestly prayer of John 17:20–22 because it is yet to be fulfilled. Jewish and gentile believers in Jesus have yet to fully become one new man in their Messiah. Jesus is Jewish and the prayers He prays from the throne room of heaven are in pure Jewish Hebraic style—with boldness and persistence. You can be sure His prayer will be answered because the Father is listening. He is simply waiting for us to obey His Word. Time is short. The three revolutions have begun. Jesus is separating the nations based on their treatment of His Jewish brethren. May we understand and embrace what Jesus is doing in this separation process and stand with Him for the sake of His people, Israel. Jesus is restoring Jews and Gentiles together as "one new man." May we fully embrace our Messianic Jewish believing brothers and sisters and heal the divide so that God's glory (kavod) might fully be imparted to the earth, opening the pathway to the final harvest. Jesus is raising up a righteous remnant of gentile Christians who will prepare humanitarian aid for Jewish people in this hour of great need—especially for those in the household of faith. May we be counted among the Righteous of the Nations who, after being confronted with the truth, respond practically to the needs of our elder brother.

May we not miss what Jesus our Jewish Messiah is doing in this hour. May we not fall asleep in the two minutes before midnight. May our lamps be filled with oil. May we lift up our eyes to heaven and proclaim the wisdom of God. May we raise our voices on earth as Yeshua's is raised in heaven: "May you restore the divide Father God! May Jew and Gentile become one. May believing Gentiles show such honor and love to their elder Jewish brothers that unbelieving Jews will become jealous unto salvation. Through the healing of this age long divide may the world believe that You sent Jesus as the Savior of the world. May Your "weighty" glory come! May it cover the earth as the waters cover the sea! May you make Jerusalem a praise in the earth. May Your Kingdom come!"

Two Minute Warning

Time has a habit of slipping away
For some it happens day after day
Until they awaken early one morning
To the alarming sound of a Two Minute Warning

People rush to set things in order
They hurriedly try to defend their border
Danger lurks on every side
The enemy is here, no place to hide

That hour is coming, don't you see
The Good Book calls it prophecy
Those not sleeping have a solution
They have embraced the three revolutions

Jew and Gentile in one accord
That's John 17 in the Holy Sword
It's not too late to participate
So trim your lamps before it's too late

Bill McCartney

EPILOGUE

Finding God's Heart in This Hour

In Matthew 7:24 Jesus taught us that whoever hears His Word and obeys it is a wise man. In John 16:13 He promised that He would send His Holy Spirit to guide us into all truth. It is through the Holy Spirit that we are able to understand Bible prophecy. It is only in the power of the Holy Spirit that we can prepare for impending struggle. This is the very foundation for the *Two Minute Warning*.

God's heart is for all believers—Jewish and gentile together in Messiah—to be bonded together in the power of the Holy Spirit. John 17:21 makes this abundantly clear. There is an interpretation obstacle here. For centuries many have misunderstood the prayer of Jesus in John 17. Clearly, Jesus prayed that Jewish believers would be in one accord with gentile believers. This restored relationship is what prompts the world to believe that Jesus is the Messiah: "That they all may be one [Jews and Gentiles who have received Jesus] as you, Father, are in Me, and I in You, that they also may be one in Us, that the world may believe that You sent me" (John 17:21).

209

This is the biblical blueprint for worldwide revival. The first century church understood and practiced this unity. That is why the gospel exploded amidst great persecution.

In Zechariah 12:3, we discover, prophetically, that every nation on earth will oppose Israel. We are presently very close to this being a reality. The *Two Minute Warning* prompts the church to rally now in anticipation of this possibility. This book serves as a clarion call to the church of the last days. A clarion call is defined as: A powerful request for action or an irresistible mandate.

The seventy-three words of Jesus' high priestly prayer in John 17 is in fact a clarion call that has for the most part gone unheeded for 1,900 years. In God's providence the time has now come when the gentile church is awakening to her prophetic mandate. There are many wonderful signs that the age long divide is being mended, and Jews and Gentiles are becoming one through Messiah. This is God's heart for the church today. As the storm clouds gather it is time for us to rally around the righteous remnant of Messianic Jewish believers. If the church prepares in advance of great persecution, there will be a wonderful harvest again—even as the struggle escalates.

A Final Challenge

from Bill McCartney

As a ministry, Promise Keepers is preparing to take the message of The Two Minute Warning around the globe. With one mighty catalytic clarion voice we desire to proclaim to the body of Christ: "Get prepared because the hour is late. It's time to honor our Jewish elder brothers and sisters before the clock runs out." I am asking you to help us carry the message of reconciliation contained in the pages of this book to the four corners of the earth. I believe the Lord has commissioned Promise Keepers to challenge the church to return to the authenticity of her early beginnings. After 1,900 years of separation between Jewish and gentile believers, the true authentic nature of the church lies dormant. It is now time to rally, awaken, and inspire the church to fulfill its end-time destiny. Notice the following sequence of events:

1. Jesus trained twelve ordinary Jewish men.
2. Over a three year period of time He explained to them from the Scriptures that He was the promised Messiah.
3. He taught these twelve ordinary Jewish men that He must die for the sins of mankind.
4. The disciples also heard him pray that Jew and Gentile would be in one accord (John 17:21).
5. These same men spoke with Him after His death and resurrection.
6. The disciples were instructed by the Lord to wait in Jerusalem until the Holy Spirit filled them, resulting in supernatural power.
7. The Holy Spirit ignited and united Jew and Gentile.
8. Persecution escalated quickly and furiously.

211

9. Jews explained the Scriptures to the Gentiles through the prompting of the Holy Spirit.

10. Through the power of the Holy Spirit, believers shared their resources and belongings as each had need. Signs, wonders, and miracles took place regularly.

11. With the possible exclusion of John the beloved, all of the disciples died as martyrs—courageously.

12. The gospel powerfully advanced.

Jesus teaches us in Matthew 24 that a day will come when a great persecution will arise that will be more severe than the early church experienced: "And you will hear of wars and rumors of wars...For nation will rise against nation, and kingdom against kingdom. And there will be famines, pestilences, and earthquakes...Then they will deliver you up to tribulation and kill you, and you will be hated by all nations for My name's sake...And many will be offended, will betray one another, and will hate one another....And because lawlessness will abound, the love of many will grow cold. But he who endures to the end shall be saved" (Matt. 24:6–7, 9–10, 12–13).

In Matthew 25, Jesus teaches three parables concerning events of the end-times. The three principles contained in these three parables were priorities within the early church. They were keys to the exponential growth and supernatural power the early church experienced. Once again, these three priorities will be marks of true authentic end-time Christianity:

1. The parable of the wise and foolish virgins: Matthew 25:1–13
   Priority: Wake up! Trim your lamps! Being filled with the Holy Spirit

2. The parable of the talents: Matthew 25:14–30
   Priority: Faithful stewardship and investing in kingdom causes

3. The parable of the sheep and goats (the judgment of the nations based on their treatment of the Jewish brethren of Jesus): Matthew 25:31–46

   Priority: Righteous gentile believers standing in unity with Jewish believers during a time of great persecution and affliction

Fulfilling the End-Time Priorities of the Lord

You might be asking: "How can I help fulfill these three end-time priorities of the Lord?" Let me give you three ways:

1. Be filled with the Holy Spirit.

It is no accident that Jesus begins his parables about the end of the age in Matthew 25 with the parable of the ten virgins. This first parable communicates the necessity of being filled with the Holy Spirit. You might say that the first parable is the foundation of the last two parables in the chapter—the talents and the sheep and goats. Ask the Holy Spirit to prepare your heart for the days ahead. In the parable of the ten virgins in Matthew 25, both the wise and the foolish virgins fell asleep before the midnight hour: "But while the bridegroom was delayed, they all slumbered and slept" (Matt. 25:5). Jesus is telling us that in the last moments of history the church will succumb to a lethargic fatigue. Ladies and gentlemen, it is now two minutes before the midnight hour. Time is short. Fill your lamps with oil! Don't be like the foolish virgins who were not prepared for the midnight cry and missed their end-time destiny. Only those who are living and walking in the power of the Holy Spirit will be ready to face the challenges ahead of us. Only those filled with the Holy Spirit will be willing to share their resources with those in need. It's only the Holy Spirit that can awaken and challenge us in this hour to love and honor the Jewish people. It is only the Holy Spirit who can heal the divide between believing Jew and Gentile after 1,900 years of separation. As well, only those living and walking in the Holy Spirit will be prepared to meet the Lord when He comes.

2. Be a faithful steward and invest in kingdom causes.

The next parable in Matthew 25 is the parable of the talents. This parable speaks of the vital importance of investing our resources in kingdom causes as we await the Lord's return. The wicked servant in the parable hid the talent that he was supposed to invest, and his lord said to him: "So you ought to have deposited my money with the bankers, and at my coming I would have received back my own with interest" (Matt. 25:27). The reason this servant did not deposit his lord's money in the bank is because he doubted in his lord's return. If there was no record of deposit in his lord's name, the money would someday belong to him if his lord failed to return. This man was not committed to his lord. Rather, he was committed to self preservation. Jesus knew that in the last days people would be lovers of money and lovers of self more than lovers of God. That is why He warns us in the parable of the talents. In these days when people seem to be committed to self preservation more than ministering to the needs of others, it will only be those who have trimmed their lamps with the oil of the Holy Spirit who will overcome the bondage of materialism. In these days when financial markets are crashing around the world, the only wise investment is in the treasury of the Lord. Here, your financial investment is protected, secure and will never decay. Consider investing in the ministry of the Road to Jerusalem (RTJ). RTJ is a partner ministry of Promise Keepers with a central goal of reconciling Jewish and gentile believers in Messiah for the salvation of Israel. There is a beautiful promise that our Lord gives at the end of the parable of the talents: "For to everyone who has, more will be given, and he will have abundance; but from him who does not have, even what he has will be taken away" (Matt. 25:29). This little word "abundance" carries the meaning of excess and fullness. In other words, Jesus is saying that when we wisely invest in His end-time kingdom causes, we personally experience exponential growth and begin to live life to the fullest. Jesus affirms this principle in Luke 6:38: "Give, and it will be given to you: good measure, pressed down, shaken together, and running over will be put into your bosom. For with the same measure that you use, it will be measured back to you."

3. Stand in unity with Jewish believers.

The third and final parable in Matthew 25 is the parable of the sheep and goats. In this parable Jesus rewards righteous Gentiles (the sheep) for their servant role in giving humanitarian aid to His end-time suffering brethren—the Jewish people. Again, without the awesome power of the Holy Spirit, Gentiles living in our day will never be inspired to lay their lives down for their Jewish brethren. For 1,900 years the message of Jew and Gentile becoming one in Jesus has been attacked by the enemy of our souls with fierce anger and great resolve. He has won most of the battles. But, things are changing! The prayer of Jesus in John chapter 17 will soon be answered! Jew and Gentile will become one in Messiah. The glory of God will come in power, and Satan's kingdom will crumble! You can help fulfill the prayer of Jesus in John 17 by giving ten copies of *Two Minute Warning* to ten people. This book is meant to educate and encourage the body of Christ. Only righteous Gentiles who stand with the brethren of Jesus during the last days will endure. Prayerfully ask the Holy Spirit to guide you as you distribute these books. As your friends and loved ones are reading *Two Minute Warning*, ask the Holy Spirit to lift 1,900 years of blindness off of their eyes. This book can only be read and understood by the power of the Holy Spirit.

ENDNOTES

CHAPTER TWO

1. Elie Wiesel, *Night* (New York: Hill and Wang, 1972, 1985), 32, 34.
2. Martin Gilbert, *The Holocaust* (New York: Henry Holt, 1985), 440–443.
3. Carol Rittner, Stephen D. Smith, Irena Steinfeldt, *The Holocaust and the Christian World* (London: Kuperard, 2000), 120.
4. Ibid., 121.
5. Ibid., 121.
6. Ibid., 123.
7. Daniel Jonah Goldhagen, *Hitler's Willing Executioners* (New York: Vintage Books, 1997), 395–396.
8. Nora Levin, *The Holocaust* (New York: Schocken Books, 1973), 265.
9. Goldhagen, *Hitler's Willing Executioners*, 386.
10. Franklin H. Littell, *The Crucifixion of the Jews* (Macon, GA: Mercer University Press, 1986, 1996), 129.
11. Richard Steigmann-Gall, *The Holy Reich* (New York: Cambridge University Press, 2003), 261–262.
12. Ibid., 27–28.
13. Goldhagen, *Hitler's Willing Executioners*, 381.
14. William Nicholls, *Christian Antisemitism: A History of Hate* (Northvale, NJ: Jason Aronson Inc., 1993), 351.
15. Goldhagen, *Hitler's Willing Executioners*, 126.
16. David I. Kertzer, *The Popes Against the Jews* (New York: Vintage Books, 2002), 206.
17. Littell, *The Crucifixion of the Jews*, 30, 49, 104.
18. Marvin R. Wilson, *Our Father Abraham* (Grand Rapids, MI: William B. Eerdmans Publishing Company, 1989), 83–84.
19. Ibid., 101.
20. Friedrich Heer, *God's First Love* (London: Phoenix, an imprint of Orion Books Ltd, 1999), 358.

21. Goldhagen, *Hitler's Willing Executioners*, 454.
22. Steigmann-Gall, *The Holy Reich*, 266–267.
23. Littell, *The Crucifixion of the Jews*, 53.
24. Ibid., 53.
25. Ibid., 70.
26. Goldhagen, *Hitler's Willing Executioners*, 107–109.
27. Ibid., 107.
28. Kertzer, *The Popes Against the Jews*, 288.
29. Heer, *God's First Love*, 336.
30. Goldhagen, *Hitler's Willing Executioners*, 110, 113.
31. Ibid., 114.
32. Littell, *The Crucifixion of the Jews*, 80.
33. Heer, *God's First Love*, 281.
34. Goldhagen, *Hitler's Willing Executioners*, 111.
35. Ibid., 437.
36. Heer, *God's First Love*, 358.
37. Goldhagen, *Hitler's Willing Executioners*, 127.
38. Ibid., 443.

CHAPTER THREE
1. "The Yellow Badge in History," Historia Judaica 4.2 (1942), 103.
2. Cited in Carol Rittner, Stephen D. Smith, and Irena Steinfeldt's *The Holocaust and the Christian World* (London: Kuperard, 2000), Opening page before table of Contents.
3. Justin Martyr, *Dialogue with Trypho, A Jew*, 29.2.
4. J. Parkes, *The Conflict of the Church and the Synagogue* (New York: Atheneum, 1969), 100.
5. Augustine, *The City of God*, 18.46.
6. Barry Horner, *Future Israel* (Nashville, TN: B&H Academic), 4–5.
7. Augustine, *Exposition on the Book of Psalms*, Vol. 5 (Oxford: John Henry Parker, 1853), 114.3.
8. Michael L. Brown, *Our Hands are Stained with Blood* (Shippensburg, PA: Destiny Image Publishers, 1992), 12–13.
9. Martin Luther, *The Jews and Their Lies* (1543).

10. Joshua Trachtenberg, *The Devil and the Jews* (Philadelphia: The Jewish Publication Society, 1983), 110.

11. Dennis Prager & Joseph Telushkin, *Why the Jews?* (New York: Touchstone, 2003), 86–87.

12. Joshua Trachtenberg, *The Devil and the Jews*, 18–20.

13. Ibid., 135, 137.

14. David I. Kertzer, *The Popes Against the Jews* (New York: Vintage Books, 2001), 96.

15. Ibid., 41.

16. Ibid., 43.

17. Ibid., 41.

18. Raul Hilberg, *The Destruction of the European Jews* (Chicago: Quadrangle, 1961), 5–6.

19. Amos Elon, *The Pity of It All* (New York: Picador, 2002), 22.

20. Ibid., 25.

21. Ibid., 400.

22. Ibid., 7.

CHAPTER FOUR

1. Franklin H. Littell, *The Crucifixion of the Jews* (Macon, GA: Mercer University Press, 1986, 1996), 109–111.

2. Melanie Phillips, *Londonistan* (New York: Encounter Books, 2006), x–xi.

3. Ibid., 139.

4. Ibid., 140.

5. Ibid., 151.

6. Ibid., 152, 155.

CHAPTER FIVE

1. Elie Wiesel, *The Town Beyond the Wall* (New York: Schocken Books, 1964), 149–151.

2. "Letter to President Bush from Evangelical Leaders," New York Times, July 29, 2007, http://www.nytimes.com/2007/07/29/us/evangelical_letter.html?_r=1&scp=1&sq=Letter%20to%20President%20Bush%20from%20Evangelical%20Leaders&st=cse.

3. Dexter Van Zile, "Mainline Churches Embrace Burge's False Narrative," *Committee for Accuracy in Middle East Reporting in America* (CAMERA), August 23, 2007, http://www.camera.org/index.asp?x_context=7&x_issue=55&x_article=1356.

4. Gary M. Burge, *Whose Land? Whose Promise?* (Cleveland, OH: The Pilgrim Press, 2003), 25.

5. The Palestinian National Charter (July 1968), Article 15.

6. Barry E. Horner, *Future Israel* (Nashville, TN: B&H Academic), 45–46.

7. Ibid., 49–50.

8. Ibid., 54.

9. G. Burge, "Christian Zionism, Evangelicals and Israel," May 2007, http://www. christian-zionism.org/article-sN.asp.

10. Ibid.

11. Burge, *Whose Land? Whose Promise?*, xi.

12. Ibid., 176–177, 179.

13. Ibid., 188.

14. Ibid., 176.

15. Raul Hilberg, *The Destruction of the European Jews* (Chicago: Quadrangle, 1961), 3–4.

16. Albertus Pieters, *The Seed of Abraham* (Grand Rapids, MI: Eerdmans, 1950), 123–124, 134.

17. O. Palmer Robertson, *The Israel of God* (Phillipsburg, NJ: P&R, 2000), 118, 121.

18. Bary Horner, *Future Israel*, 57.

CHAPTER SIX

1. The Barna Group, The Barna Update, "New Marriage and Divorce Statistics," March 31, 2008, http://www.barna.org, (accessed February 20, 2009).

2. Marvin R. Wilson, *Our Father Abraham* (Grand Rapids, MI: Wm. B. Eerdmans Publishing Company, 1989), 201.

3. Ibid., 202

4. Maurice Lamm, *The Jewish Way in Love and Marriage* (Middle Village, NY: Jonathan David Publishers, Inc., 1980, 1991), 11–13.

5. David C. and Esther R. Gross, *Under the Wedding Canopy* (New York: Hippocrene Books, 1996), 10.

6. Ibid., 17.

7. Ibid., 18.

8. Sally Ann Berk, *Jewish Wit and Wisdom* (New York: Black Dog & Leventhal Publishers, 2000), 136–153.

9. Andrew Vachss, "You Carry the Cure in Your Own Heart," *Parade*, August 28, 1994.

10. Aaron Fruh, *The Forgotten Blessing* (Grand Rapids, MI: Chosen Books, 2006), 103.

11. George Barna, *Transforming Children Into Spiritual Champions* (Ventura, CA: Regal Books, 2003), 77–79.

CHAPTER SEVEN

1. Art Katz, *The Mystery of Israel and the Church* (artkatzministries.org/ online_ bookstore), Chapter 9.

CHAPTER EIGHT

1. Rabbi Joseph Telushkin, *Jewish Wisdom* (New York: William Morrow, 1994), 498.

2. Leslie B. Flynn, *What the Church Owes the Jew* (Carlsbad, CA: Magnus Press, 1998), 2.

CHAPTER NINE

1. United States Holocaust Memorial, online Holocaust Encyclopedia, s.v. "Elizabeth Koenig Kaufman," http://www.ushmm.org/wlc/article. php?lang=en&ModuleId= 10007518, (accessed February 20, 2009).

2. Elie Wiesel, *Night* (New York: Hill and Wang, 1972, 1985), Preface, xv.

3. Ibid., 118–120.

CHAPTER TEN

1. Ron Rosenbaum, *Those Who Forget the Past* (New York: Random House, 2004), 491.

2. John Hagee, *In Defense of Israel* (Lake Mary, FL: Frontline, 2007), 137–140.

3. John Hagee, *Jerusalem Countdown* (Lake Mary, FL: Frontline, 2006), 175.

4. Ibid., 176–177.

ABOUT THE AUTHORS

COACH BILL MCCARTNEY - Former head football coach of the University of Colorado, Coach Bill McCartney is the founder, CEO and Chairman of the Board of Promise Keepers.

He is also the founder and chairman of The Road to Jerusalem ministry. The organization's mission is to encourage Gentile believers in Jesus Christ to embrace the Messianic Jewish community.

Coach "Mac" led the University of Colorado to a share of the national championship in 1990. He is a member of the Orange Bowl Hall of Fame and the Colorado Sports Hall of Fame, and was honored as Big Eight Conference Coach of the Year in 1985, 1989, and 1990. He won National Coach of the Year honors in 1989.

He is the author of four books, *Ashes to Glory*, *Sold Out*, *Sold Out Two-gether* with Lyndi McCartney, and *Blind Spots*.

Coach "Mac" lives with his wife, Lyndi, in Westminster, CO. The McCartneys have four grown children: Mike, Tom, Kristyn, and Marc, and ten grandchildren.

AARON DAVID FRUH is Lead Pastor of Knollwood Church in Mobile, Alabama. He is involved in humanitarian work in Israel. He holds an M.A. from Wheaton College Graduate School. Aaron has authored two other books: *The Decree of Esther* and *The Forgotten Blessing*, both published by Baker Publishing Group. Aaron and his wife Sharon have four children: Rachel, Elizabeth, Hannah and Nathan.